Just Add H$_2$Oh!

A Recipe for Hydronic Marketing Success

DAN HOLOHAN

In memory of Edward Joseph Holohan, a fighter

1920-1997

"People are always going to need heat,
especially in the winter."

Thanks, Dad.

On November 23, 1996, The Lovely Marianne and our three high-school-age daughters, Meghan, Colleen and Erin, visited our eldest daughter, Kelly, who was a freshman at a magical place called the University of Notre Dame. It was Parents Weekend and we had tickets for the football game against Rutgers. This was Coach Lou Holtz's last home game ever in the old Notre Dame stadium that Knute Rockne had built. Beginning in 1997, there would be over 20,000 additional seats and all sorts of new amenities. The end of two eras.

During the game, and quite spontaneously, a wave started to roll from one section of the stadium to the next. In a moment it was pounding around and around the stadium, and attracting more interest than the game. As each group stood, they shouted LOU! It was an incredible sight, but as it turned out, it was only the beginning. A *second* wave started, just as spontaneously a few minutes after the first - but this one went in the opposite direction. These people also cheered LOU!

As the two waves converged, they became one for a moment, and then they continued on in their independent and opposite directions for a full five minutes. It was as if some new organism had been born. People were crying with glee at such a beautiful sight. Kelly told me later that the students had been trying to do this all year long, but were not successful until that day. "But we just kept *trying*,

Dad! We *never* gave up," she said. "Even though a lot of people said we couldn't do it, we just *never* gave up."

I raised her to be that way, and I'm so proud of her.

This book is for people who *never* give up.

Dan Holohan

Final Score

Notre Dame 62

Rutgers 0

Wet Head:

A wildly enthusiastic person who is biased toward the best, who honestly believes that people will buy *value*, not price, if value is properly presented in a way that is in the customer's self-interest.

List of Ingredients

1

The Most Impressive Sale of All Time

I was talking to a guy who was frustrated because he hadn't been able to convince a customer to buy what he wanted to sell him, which was hydronic heat. "It was so frustrating," he said. "He just looked at my price and said he wasn't interested. I love hydronic heat, and I'd like to sell more of it. That would be great for my business, but I think it's just too hard to sell."

"You think?" I said.

"Yeah," he said, nodding in a resigned way.

"I can tell you about a guy who made a *much* harder sale," I said.

"Harder than what *I* was up against?"

"Much, *much* harder," I promised him. "In fact, this guy had to make the toughest sale of all time. He had to sell people on changing a habit they'd had for thousands of years."

"Who was this guy?" he asked.

"His name was Sanford Fleming," I said.

"Never heard of him."

An Idea Whose Time Had Come

You've probably never heard of him either. He became a Dead Man long before you were born, but when he was alive he lived with a passion that burned brightly. He filled each day with an enthusiasm that was positively contagious. He was a master of persuasion because he approached *everything* he did with other people's best interests in mind.

When you click the TV remote to an away ball game, you should thank Sanford Fleming.

When you walk onto an airplane, you should think of Sanford Fleming.

When you talk to a faraway friend on the telephone, you should consider Sanford Fleming.

You should sing the praises of Sanford Fleming because he changed the way the entire world thinks. And he wasn't a scientist, or a preacher, or a politician; he was a simple railroad engineer. One day he got it in his head that he should form a company and build a railroad from one end of Canada to the other. He got this idea in the mid-1800s, and if you look at an atlas of the world you can see what a passionate guy Sanford Fleming really was. Canada is a *very* big, *very* cold place.

The problem Sanford Fleming had, though, was *time*. Not the *length* of time, but the way people were deciding what time it was at any given place. Just over 100 years ago, people set their clocks by the position of the sun, and that was fine if you planned to stay in one place your entire life. But Sanford Fleming wanted to build a very long railroad, and he wanted to make it run on time. So the way people were dealing with time just wouldn't do.

And being a passionate man, he set out to change things.

Now, here's what Sanford Fleming was facing. When it was noon in Toronto, Canada, it was 12:25 in Montreal, 344 miles to the east. At that same instant, it was also 12:08 in Belleville, Ontario, which was 114 miles to the east. And it was 11:58 in Hamilton, just 44 miles to the west. There were 100 similar time zones in the United States. Left this way, no one would ever catch the right train.

Sanford Fleming got it through his head that there should be uniform time zones all around the globe so that he could build his railroad and print a schedule that made sense. Here's what he was looking to set up:

Pacific Standard Time

Mountain Standard Time

Central Standard Time

Eastern Standard Time

Atlantic Standard Time

Aleutian Standard Time

Yukon Standard Time

Newfoundland Standard Time

North American (3) Standard Time

North American (9) Standard Time

South American Standard Time

Eastern Brazil Standard Time

Western Brazil Standard Time

Trinity of Acre Standard Time

Fernando De Noronha Standard Time

Chilean Standard Time

Middle European Time

East European Standard Time

Greenwich Mean Time

Add to this short list an additional 36 time zones and you'll get a sense of the way Sanford Fleming's imagination zigzagged around the globe. Imagine if you left your home tomorrow morning with an idea such as this. Where would you begin? Who would you speak to first? People would think you were out of your mind, wouldn't they?

But that didn't concern Sanford Fleming. Unless he got time straightened out, he couldn't run his railroad. And he *really* wanted that railroad.

Well, you probably never heard of him. And even if you have heard of him, I'm sure you don't give him much thought. But you know what? He succeeded. And the reason he succeeded was that there is nothing more powerful that an idea whose time has come. In just a few years, Sanford Fleming managed to convince all the governments of the world to adopt standard time. They did so - all together and at the same moment - on November 17, 1883. And keep in mind this was not an easy thing to do back in the late-1800s. The average person on the street believed Sanford Fleming was messing around with *God's* time.

But he convinced them anyway because he refused to give up. He built his railroad, and when he was through with that magnificent labor, he designed the first Canadian postage stamp. The Queen of England made him a knight. And then he became a Dead Man.

But you should take a moment to remember him. And you should thank him when you watch that TV show, or walk onto that plane, or call your friend long distance.

And you should remember Sir Sanford if your customer tells you your price for that well-designed hydronic system is too high. Sir Sanford changed the way the whole world viewed time by presenting people with positively irresistible *benefits*. You can do the same.

As a Wet Head, you can do *great* things. You can convince people they should make an investment in their comfort. You can build as much excitement and anticipation around their new hydronic heating system as the landscaper manages to build around their new lawn and those expensive bushes. And don't tell me the people won't go for it because the neighbors can't *see* the hydronics. They sure can *feel* the hydronics. There are five senses, you know. You get to smell that steak before you get to taste it, don't you?

Oh, I *know* you can do amazing things, but you first have to believe in your goals. Here, consider this.

Rising to New Heights

I believe you can achieve *anything* you set out to do as long as your goal is reasonable and you *really* believe you can do it. I've given up hope of ever becoming the heavyweight champion of the world - even though I'm the same age as Big George Foreman. That's not a reasonable goal for me.

But wanting to convince people that they will be happier and more comfortable if they have hydronic heat in their homes certainly is a reasonable goal. You have all the facts on your side; all you really have to do is put together a plan and get enthusiastic. Enthusiasm is positively contagious!

I know this is true because The Lovely Marianne and I started this company of ours in 1989 after watching this Nike sneaker commercial. We kept trying to decide whether I should quit the good job I had at the time and strike out on our own. More than anything, I wanted to be a writer who specializes in hydronic heating. Nearly everyone we talked to said this was a stupid idea. "You'll never make a living," they said. "You have so much time in your job. Why lose all that security?"

I have to admit, their arguments were good ones. We had four small daughters, a mortgage, a car loan, and less than $5,000 in savings. The Lovely hadn't been employed since our first daughter, Kelly, was born, and Marianne's skill as a computer key-punch operator wasn't much in demand anymore.

But I wanted to be a writer who specialized in hydronics, and I kept hearing that Nike commercial. Just Do It, it said. Just . . . Do . . . It.

So we Did It. And we have been on an exhilarating roller coaster ride ever since. We've had fun, we've traveled all over the world, we've met people who have become dear friends, we've made a good living, and we've never felt more alive.

Everything worked out.

Sometimes you Just Do It.

You don't listen to people who tell you what can't be done.

When someone tells you hydronic heat is too expensive, you have to persuade them that they're not seeing the full picture. When they ask, "Well, what about air-conditioning?" you explain that air-conditioning is a wonderful thing, and you'll be happy to install one of those systems for them as well. You get past their negativity by staying positive.

You can achieve anything as long as your goal is reasonable, you have a plan, and you believe in what you're doing.

There were many people who believed the Empire State Building would never rise, but it did, and quickly! Do you know how long it took to build this magnificent building? Nineteen months.

Now, I want you to appreciate that this building soars 1,250 feet above New York's Fifth Avenue. For many years it was the tallest building in the world. Yet it took just 19 months to build, and that included the time required to clear the site. Before they could start the Empire State Building they had to knock down and get rid of the debris from the old Waldorf-Astoria Hotel, which had stood on that site since 1897. They began demolition of the hotel on October

1, 1929. By September 1, 1930, just 11 months later, they had the steel beams, girders and columns for the Empire State completely erected. Eight months after that, on May 1, 1931, the new tenants moved into the tallest building in the world.

Nineteen months.

Many people said this couldn't be done, but they Just Did It.

Ask a negative person how long it would take to build the Empire State Building nowadays and they'll hang their heads and tell you it will take at least 19 months to complete the preliminary environmental-impact study on where the building's shadow will fall. And then they'll hire a thousand lawyers and *never* get done.

The Dead Men who built the steam-heated Empire State Building broke free of the herd, made a decision, refused to listen to anyone who said it couldn't be done, and they Just Did It.

You can do *anything* you set out to do, as long as your goal is reasonable, and as long as you believe you can do it.

Biased Toward The Best

For years, I've watched my friend Alan Levi, Ace Troubleshooter, sell replacement steam boilers with two low-water cutoffs instead of one. "How do you do that?" I ask. "I just tell the customer that this is what they get from me," he says with a smile. "I explain that my price is higher than my competitor's because I'm doing a better job of protecting their new-boiler investment. Low-water cutoffs are less expensive than boilers. It's like wearing a belt and suspenders. It's obvious." He smiles again. "Dan, my customers expect *me* to be the expert. I just give them what's in their best interest."

I've watched Alan sell $40,000 hydronic radiant heating systems using the same technique - and he does this here on Long Island where competition is savage, and consumers are both smart and wary. I've come to realize that Alan succeeds because he's doing something most heating contractors <u>aren't</u> doing.

Alan is a Wet Head. He is biased toward the best. He will always "sell up." He sells value over low price. He's wildly enthusiastic. He presents his case *totally* in the customer's self-interest, and he is *very* successful.

In my travels around the country, I've seen other Wet Heads do what Alan does. They're all biased toward the best. They deliver superb hydronic heating systems.

They are financially successful <u>and</u> they're having fun.

I've watched these people carefully for years. I've listened to their success stories. I've met their delighted customers. I've seen the similarity these companies have with successful companies of the past. And I've noticed that there's a common thread running through all of these successful companies.

These people are using a recipe. And it all begins with this first ingredient.

Defining the Business You're *Really* In

Every week, usually on Monday, I have a meeting with myself. I go someplace where it's quiet for 20 minutes or so, and I think about what business I'm really in. I do this because the world is changing so quickly. Once a week, for 20 minutes, I think about whether my business is heading in the right direction.

While I'm thinking about my own business, I often think about other businesses as well. For instance, have you ever wondered why railroad executives, maybe even someone like Sir Sanford Fleming, never invested in airplanes way back when? That would seem like a natural extension for someone in the transportation business, wouldn't it? I mean, if you were in the business of quickly getting people from one place to another, you'd be interested in flying machines, wouldn't you?

But as it turned out, the railroad executives *didn't* invest in airplanes. You know why? Because they weren't *really* in the business of quickly getting people from one place to another. They were in the *railroad* business. That's the way they saw themselves - as railroad men. They were in the business of perpetuating what they happened to be doing.

Those guys *fought* the airlines.

They told the American people that airlines were unsafe and expensive. Why, you'd have to be nuts to fly!

They sat around and told each other that the American public would *never* fly. "People will just keep doing what they're doing," they told each other. "We have nothing to fear from airplanes. We run the transportation in this country."

Because they once thought this way, they no longer run the transportation in this country.

Picture This

The folks at Kodak didn't invent the Polaroid camera, you know. You would think they would have because, in those days, who knew more about cameras than Kodak?

The way I figure it, the Kodak people didn't invent the Polaroid camera because Kodak had a huge investment in making *their* sort of camera, and in film processing. They had all those film-developing labs. They had all those people opening the mail, taking out those rolls of film and turning them into prints.

"Who the heck would want instant photographs?" they said to each other. They really thought they were in the photography business.

Kodak didn't invent the camcorder either.

But on the other hand, even though the people at Polaroid made instant pictures, they didn't invent the photocopy machine. They didn't make this technological leap because they thought they were in the instant *photography* business. They figured making copies was the business of the mimeograph people.

But the mimeograph people didn't invent the photocopy machine either. The mimeograph guys probably saw those first Xerox boxes as expensive toys that no one would *ever* buy. Who would spend all that money when they could get cheap copies from a mimeograph machine?

When was the last time you used *your* mimeograph machine?

How about your slide rule? And by the way, why didn't the slide rule people invent the hand-held electronic calculator? Do you suppose they might have had too much invested in the slide rule business?

The folks who were making the photocopy machines didn't think to invent the fax machine, which shouldn't surprise you at this point. It probably didn't occur to them because they were so darn busy building and selling photocopy machines.

Notice how the people who make the breakthroughs are rarely the people who are currently involved in that particular business.

Why didn't the phone company invent the cellular phone?

Why didn't the US Postal Service invent Federal Express? Uh . . . never mind.

Here, this is better: Why didn't the farmers invent the grocery store? You would think the idea would have occurred to the farmers, wouldn't you? I mean, after all, they had all the food, didn't they? They needed a place to sell it, and what better place than a grocery store?

No, it took The Great Atlantic and Pacific *Tea* Company - a company that had nothing to do with food or farming - to invent the grocery store. I think they saw the opportunity because they were standing on the outside, looking in.

You Wanna Super Size It?

But then again, the A&P didn't invent *fast* food, did they? They had all this food in all these stores. They had people coming in day after day to buy that food. But apparently, it never dawned on them to cook some of that food and sell it to the people who were already there. Some of those people must have been hungry. Wouldn't you think?

No, the A&P was into *slow* food, not fast food. So who invented the fast food? It wasn't McDonald's. Nah, those brothers owned a single restaurant. They sold burgers and thick shakes. It never occurred to them to franchise the thing. They had no vision of Ronald McDonald dancing in their heads.

It took a blender salesman, Roy Kroc, to see the opportunity. He stopped by to visit the McDonald brothers one day, saw the possibilities, bought the name and the idea from them, and built one of the most profitable businesses ever.

Think about the heating business for a moment. The coal companies didn't invent the oil burner. You know why? They had this huge investment in mining coal. They saw oil as a threat. They were so busy doing what they did from day to day that they never saw the big picture.

The Problem With Inertia

I think all these people could have profited by taking a 20-minute, Monday morning meeting with themselves. "What business am I *really* in?" they could have asked.

I think a lot of companies get stuck because they have an investment in their own inertia. They're afraid to stop the ball from rolling in that particular direction.

Which, I figure, is why the copper-fin-tube radiation manufacturers didn't invent the copper-fin-tube boiler. It's also why it didn't occur to these guys to get into the hydronic radiant-heating business as leaders instead of as followers. Baseboard people saw hydronic radiant tubing as a threat to their business, rather than as an extension. They tried to stop it, but there is nothing more powerful - or unstoppable - than an idea whose time has come.

Why didn't the people who make the air scoops invent something like the Spirovent? I remember talking to an air scoop manufacturer when the Spirovent first showed up. "Contractors will never pay that much," he said. "Besides, look at the thing. It has a screen. That's bound to clog. Contractors will never buy it. It costs too much, and it's bound to cause trouble."

I still see that guy. He's trying to catch up with Spirovent as I write this. He didn't even know what the "screen" was. He couldn't see the brilliance of his competitor because he was too busy making what he made. He needed to step back and *see*.

Spirovents sold because they *really* worked. As soon as the Wet Heads learned this, they bought the thing in great quantity - even though it cost more. Wet Heads have no problem selling a more expensive item. They learn how it can benefit the customer, and then they do a great job of telling that story.

It's not easy to recognize and accept change. You have to step outside your business to see things clearly. You have to look at the world through your customer's eyes. You have to see - truly *see* - what they need. You have to run toward their problems because within every one of their problems you will find a business.

For instance, are your customers uncomfortable? Are they dissatisfied with the service they receive? Are they concerned about health issues? Do they hesitate to spend their money because they don't perceive enough value in dealing with a heating contractor?

What are they thinking? What are their problems? And what are you doing to find out about those problems?

Running Toward Problems

I notice from looking in my newspaper that the folks who run Macy*s, the department store chain, are now in the duct-cleaning business. Someone in upper management at Macy*s must have looked around and realized that the majority of Americans are choking and gagging on the stuff that's spewing from millions of filthy scorched air ducts.

Maybe that person lives with a furnace and figures other Americans must be as miserable as she is.

So she started a service, and ran this ad in the paper.

Notice how they do this. They show a photo of a serious, clean-cut young man about to stick a vacuum hose into the living room register. See how the only tool visible in the photo is a screw driver? Makes the process look simple, doesn't it? The clean-cut guy is kneeling next to what appears to be a very expensive grandfather clock. He hasn't knocked it over and that proves he's not a moron. Macy*s recognizes that many of their customers think less-than-favorable thoughts about service people. Ah, but *this* guy you can trust around your good stuff! It's subtle, but it works.

Look at the way they focus on the *benefits* of what they're going to do for people. Macy*s is a very big, very old, and very successful store. A big part of their success, I believe, comes from the way they recognize the difference between a feature (which most contractors fall in love with) and a benefit (which is what people buy).

The benefits of having clean ducts?

- Helps relieve symptoms of allergies, asthma and other respiratory discomfort.

- Helps reduce your winter heating costs.

Macy*s is offering three things they know will get their customers' attention - health, comfort and economy.

So you're a Wet Head. But are you offering benefits such as these when you're selling a hydronic heating system? Or are you just selling a boiler, or some brand of radiation. And before you answer, keep in mind nobody ever bought a boiler because they wanted to own a boiler. They wanted to own what the boiler *does*. See the difference? As a Wet Head, it's your job to tell them what a boiler does. And don't tell them a boiler heats water; that's a *feature*. Concentrate instead on the benefits.

Boilers keep babies warm.

Think about it.

In their ad, Macy*s describes the duct-cleaning process in terms regular human beings can understand. They mention that they use patented industrial grade equipment. I'm not sure what that means, but it sound like that machine will kick the snot out of the dirt, doesn't it? It sounds tough.

They also mention that their equipment is fitted with HEPA filters, which nobody understands, and they know this. That's why, through a footnote, they explain that a HEPA filter will trap particles as small as 1/300th of a human hair, and will filter 99.97% of the dirt, dirt and irritants found indoors.

They're using a comparison anybody can understand. Everyone knows how tiny a human hair is. Imagine something 300 times tinier! Intentionally or not, Macy*s is also playing on the well-known theme of Ivory Soap (99-44/100% pure). Macy*s HEPA filter keeps things cleaner than Ivory Soap!

I just looked in my local Yellow Pages to see how a scorched-air heating contractor who is also in the duct cleaning business might compete with the likes of Macy*s.

The guy with the largest advertisement lists his company's name and telephone number and then these items:

- Air Testing

- Sanitizing

- Fire

- Puffback

- Mold/Bacteria

- Ventilating Ducts

- Musty Odors

These aren't even features. They're items, events and procedures. If you were a home owner, whose ad would look better to you? The one from Macy*s or this one?

No one ever bought a boiler because they wanted to own a boiler. Look for the problem, run toward it, and then focus on the *benefits* your customer will get by buying your solution.

The Asbestos Opportunity

When asbestos became a health issue many heating contractors shied away from jobs that had asbestos because they didn't know how to deal with it. "We'll be happy to replace that boiler and those pipes, but you'll have to get someone to remove that nasty asbestos first," they'd say to the customer.

The customer, not knowing which way to turn, might have decided to keep the old boiler for another year. But if the boiler was shot, the customer probably asked around and then hired an asbestos abatement company.

Now suppose that abatement company had a reciprocal agreement with some smart Wet Head heating contractor. "You recommend me and I'll recommend you." There's a good chance the smart Wet Head is going to get that boiler job, right?

Rather than see asbestos as a problem, a smart Wet Head will either enter the abatement business or form an alliance with a company that specializes in it. Mutual recommendations can go a long way toward making two businesses grow.

So are you working with a local asbestos guy? And if not, why not?

Now think about this. Once the asbestos is removed, who is going to install the new insulation? If the customer has steam heat, someone had better insulate those old pipes. If they're left bare the steam will condense in the basement instead of in the upstairs radiators. The new boiler won't get the job done, and you'll be left holding the bag.

The customer might balk at paying for new insulation. After all, he just paid to have the asbestos removed! But a Wet Head will explain that there was a reason for asbestos in the first place. He might compare a bare pipe to a paper coffee cup. Then he'll compare an insulated pipe to a Thermos bottle. He'll ask the customer which he would use if he was trying to keep that coffee warm for a long time.

Wet Heads always make connections to things regular human beings can understand.

Wet Heads will see the opportunity insulation presents and either get into the business, or work with a company that does this work. Wet Heads network.

High-efficiency boilers often don't get along with old chimneys. The cold masonry can make the products of combustion condense into an acidic brew inside the chimney. This isn't a problem; it's a great opportunity to sell chimney liners or direct-vent boilers.

Some contractors will tell the customer, "You'd better do something about that old chimney." A Wet Head, on the other hand, will seize the opportunity and increase the sale by using a plain-English explanation of the problem followed by an easy-to-understand solution. A Wet Head will combine the *benefits* of high-efficiency and safety.

Those Beautiful Buried Fuel Oil Tanks !

Where I live on Long Island, New York, nearly everyone heats their homes with No. 2 fuel oil. Some of my neighbors have houses with basements, and that's where you'll find the oil tanks. Most of these tanks hold 275 gallons of No. 2 fuel oil.

I live in a house that has no basement. When we bought this house back in 1978 it had a steel, 275-gallon oil tank buried under my front lawn. It wasn't that deep; the top of the tank was no more than two feet below the surface. I never gave it much thought, other than to make sure the cap was always on the fill pipe. I didn't want rain to get into my buried tank because water is heavier than fuel oil. It sinks to the bottom of the tank and causes all sorts of service problems.

I have thousands and thousands of neighbors here on Long Island, and they all have buried oil tanks. Not long ago, everyone began to worry what would happen if these tanks sprung leaks. You see, we get our drinking water from an aquifer under the ground. If oil were to seep into our drinking water there's no telling what would happen. We might even get nastier than we already are.

The oil companies that deliver No. 2 fuel oil to the tens of thousands of people who have buried oil tanks had cause to worry. They were concerned that if their customers had their buried oil tanks removed, they would also switch to natural gas. The gas company sells the gas, and they have lots of money available to tell home owners about what they gleefully called the "time bombs" buried under their lawns.

Some oil dealers responded to the challenge by imitating ostriches. They stuck their heads in the ground - right down there with those buried tanks.

Other oil companies saw the opportunity and seized it. They went into the tank-replacement business. They also worked with tank-testing companies and, in some case, environmental clean-up companies. Some fuel oil dealers even banded together to form an insurance company that covered any customer who might have a leaking tank (an expensive proposition for the home owner).

They had a lemon, but they turned it into lemonade. The saw the problem, and then instead of running from it, they ran toward it and discovered a new business. Pretty smart, eh?

What Happened to Mom and Pop

Let's stay on Long Island for a minute. We have all this oil heat, right? There used to be hundreds of little companies, most started after World War II by families who canvassed the new communities the tract-housing developers were spitting out. Mom and Pop fuel oil dealer did a wonderful job of delivering oil and taking care of problems that popped up from year to year.

They got into a routine, and after a while, they forgot to tell their customers what they, the oil companies, were doing for them. They began to think of the customer as just that - a customer, someone who would buy from them no matter what.

They stopped telling their story. They stopped adding value to the service they offered.

Out of nowhere, fuel oil cooperatives formed and stole the lunch of the Mom and Pop fuel oil dealers. The people who ran the cooperatives put together slick mailers that asked the home owners why they were paying so much for oil. "What's Mom and Pop doing for you?" they asked. And since it had been years since Mom and Pop had spoken, many customers couldn't come up with a reason - other than habit - to explain why they were doing what they were doing.

Mom and Pop may not have been offering the best of service.

Mom and Pop's price was higher than the cooperative's price.

Mom and Pop didn't know the first thing about how to add value to what they had to offer.

The cooperatives saw what was happening and they monopolized on it. People didn't feel anything other than ambivalence toward their fuel oil suppliers. That was the fuel oil dealer's problem, and the cooperative's opportunity - all at the same time.

When you don't convince people of your value, they will always shop for bargains.

Which Might Explain Why There Are So Many Home Depots

Give me an hour to drive in any direction here on Long Island and I'll find you at least 10 great big Home Depot stores. We have a lot of these home centers because we have a lot of people here on Long Island, and they're all looking for a bargain.

Home Depot opens early in the morning and stays open until very late at night. They greet you at the door with a big hello. They help you pick stuff out. They show you how to do it yourself. They even give you a hand loading your car. They wave as you drive away. They offer credit cards and they advertise everywhere.

The great big Home Depot is there because home owners like bargains. They like to save money, and they think they can do things just as well as any contractor (look at how many do-it-yourself books and TV shows there are). Home owners think these thoughts *because not enough contractors have impressed upon them that the professional services they offer have real value.*

When you don't convince people of your value, they will always shop for bargains.

And this is why Home Depots are sprouting like pimples on prom night all across the land. The Home Depot folks saw the problem contractors were having selling the value of what they do, and they created a business around it. "You don't need a contractor," they say. "We can show you how to do what they do just as well by yourself. In fact, many of our employees are former contractors!"

Ever listen to those guys in the aisles? There's a *reason* why they're former contractors.

Wet Heads design and install systems you will never find in the aisles of the Home Depot or any other American home center. Then they do a great job of getting the word out.

Wet Heads recognize the Home Depot for what it really is - a multimillion dollar solution to meek contractors who haven't done a good job of telling their story.

Wet Heads run *toward* problems, and *become* the contractors who add value to their customers' lives.

Do You Think People Are Comfortable With Their Heating Systems?

You're a Wet Head so you're probably finely tuned into the Great Indoors. When I walk into a room, I look immediately for the radiators, the ductwork, anything that has to do with heating. The Lovely Marianne sees this as a sickness; I view it as a sport.

I'm constantly visiting buildings that have scorched air heat, and believe me, the people who have to live or work in these buildings are miserable. The temperature swings like a pendulum. The air is much too hot and dry. There are drafts everywhere. The systems are noisy. The people seem to suffer from more respiratory ailments. They're miserable.

And in most cases, they don't know things can be better. They're living in abnormal circumstances, which they consider to be normal.

There's your opportunity. You can tell them about something that's better. You can solve every comfort-related problem they have. And you *can* get your price.

But you have to be able to tell your story better than anyone else, so now I'm going to show you just how to do that.

3

Dead Men Marketing

In 1934 the May Oil Burner Company put together a presentation book for their salespeople to use. It was made from high-quality paper (still looks good after all these years!) and contained 30 pages. It was 10-1/2 inches wide and 15-1/2 inches high. It's title was *The Home of Heart's Desire*.

I came across this treasure in an old book store in Portsmouth, New Hampshire a few years back and I've been learning lessons from it ever since.

The May Oil Burner company made an oil burner they called Quiet May. This was during the time when just about everyone burned coal. The company had an uphill fight because people were so used to having coal bins and getting coal delivered by clattering coal trucks. People were also used to dirty basements, and the rigors of shoveling coal every day. They thought this was normal.

The May Oil Burner company set out to change people's habits, and they did it in a classic way. They presented a persuasive argument that was in the customer's self-interest. They organized their thoughts, and then they sold people not an oil burner, but intangibles such as health, cleanliness, time, family togetherness, peace of mind, love and friendship.

And you thought an oil burner was just an oil burner?

I'm going to show you some pages from this wonderful little book. I'd like you to think about what they're selling, and I'd like you to contrast what they did with what you're doing today. See if your approach is anything like theirs.

Listen to the way they invite you in, all the while speaking of intangibles such as protective love, a woman's touch, the laughter of children, the camaraderie of friendships.

Heck of a way to introduce an oil burner, eh?

THE HOME
OF
HEART'S DESIRE

Among the home makers of America, whether modest or affluent, there is an ever-increasing trend toward the home livable - the home healthful - the home beautiful. Home life at its best reflects the protective love of the head of the house - the deft touch of a woman's hand, the laughter of children and the camaraderie of friendships. In inviting you to come with us through "The Home of Heart's Desire", we do so with the sincere hope and belief that we can contribute in no small measure to the attainment of your home-making ideals.

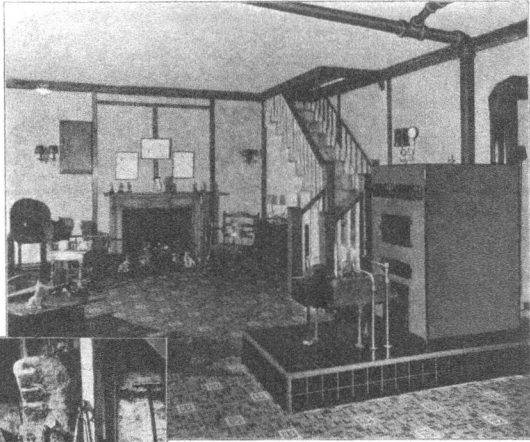

An extra room at no extra cost

No more of this!

*T*he installation of a QUIET MAY made this additional living space available at no extra cost. Twenty-five percent of the investment in a home is generally below the first floor. Why not convert it to useful or pleasurable purposes and enjoy it to the utmost?

Pictured and described herein are extra dividends in the way of ease, comfort, cleanliness and economy that make the installation of The QUIET MAY Oil Heating System one of the most satisfactory investments you can make in your home.

Here they move to something more concrete - additional living space. How do you suppose that photo of the new den struck someone who had been shoveling coal in a dark basement back in 1934?

The effect of fluctuating temperature on family health and happiness is very marked. Colds and attendant respiratory troubles, due largely to varying house temperatures, are said to be responsible for at least one-third of a family's doctor bills. The cost in terms of reduced personal efficiency is incalculable. Children, who do most of their playing on the floor where temperature fluctuations are greatest, pay especially heavy penalties, very often with serious results. Rarely is heat from a coal-fired furnace just right. Except, for short periods, when the temperature is on its way upward or downward, it is either too cold or too warm. QUIET MAY'S automatic controls maintain an even temperature at all times. They never take a day off. They never forget.

Put the kid in the photo and then talk about his health and the cost of doctors. Consider how many children were dying from common diseases during the 1930s. What an impact this must have made on a prospective customer!

A QUIET MAY *owner writes, "There are only two
reasons why anybody would be without a* QUIET
MAY. *Either they don't know its advantages or else they
are deluded with the idea that they can't afford it. It is our
experience that the thrifty homeowner can't afford* not *to own
it. Our budget book shows that* QUIET MAY *heat costs us
very much less than coal heat. A friend of ours who formerly
heated with gas, now has a* QUIET MAY *and has cut his
fuel bill in half without sacrificing a single thing that gas heat
afforded."* He *concludes by saying, "I guess a lot of people have
the same ideas about oil burners that I had before I owned
a* QUIET MAY. *I had been told about soot - with* QUIET
MAY *there is no soot! I had been told about oil odor! There
is no odor with* QUIET MAY. *Noise? There is no noise with*
QUIET MAY!

"You can't afford *not* to own one." Keep this in mind
later when we're looking at how a hydronic radiant system
pays for itself in fuel savings.

They also confront the issues of soot, odor, and noise.
They bring them up before the customer can and try to
dispel concerns about oil heat.

*I*t isn't very pleasant, is it, to have everything spick and span, then have to run down the cellar to give "old man furnace" a much needed poke, only to return with coal-besmudged hands and a trail of cellar-soiled foot prints. In "The Home of Heart's Desire" there's nothing like that to contend with! No coal or ash dust to seep up through the house. No coal dirt to ruin clothes, rugs or drapes. No besmeared walls. No fire to build. No ashes to put out. QUIET MAY homes don't have to be repainted so often. QUIET MAY homes don't have to be redecorated so often. QUIET MAY heat is clean heat. QUIET MAY cellars are clean cellars. QUIET MAY homes are clean homes.

Notice how they identify the problems they *know* the prospective customer is having, and then offer their product as the solution. These guys have done their research!

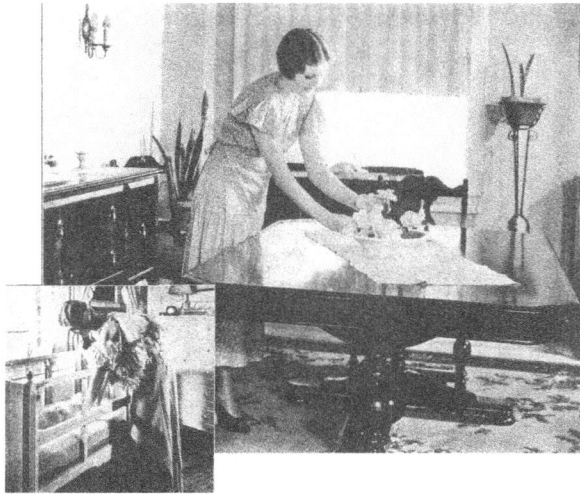

*T*he stage is all set, even to the last deft touch. Plenty of time to relax - do a bit of shopping - read a book - romp with the kiddies or maybe take-in a picture before the menfolks get home or guests arrive for dinner and an evening of bridge. Getting up early in the morning to fire-up is now but reminiscent of other days. Up and down cellar steps throughout the day and dashing down the last thing at night to "throw on" the final quota is no longer in the scheme of things. QUIET MAY is not comparatively quiet, but actually quiet. Hours of unnecessary toil, together with the coal-consuming, ash-belching cellar demon, pass out the door when QUIET MAY comes in.

Since the woman was usually the one who tended the coal boiler, they paint a word picture that's very appealing to her.

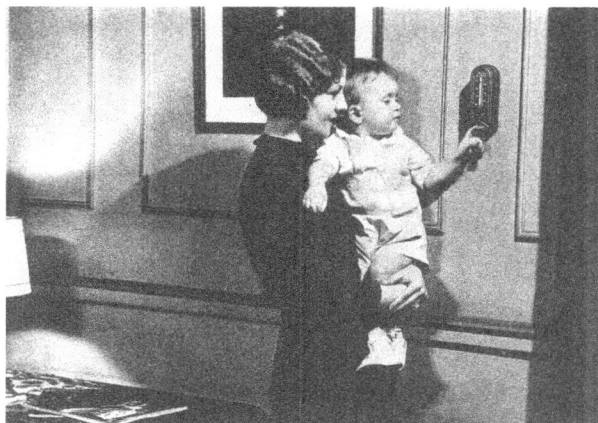

*T*he QUIET MAY *is the choice of emperor, prince and potentate, but it is equally a fact that scores thousands of homes that must run on very modest incomes* heat *with* QUIET MAY, *for the simple reason that it is the* most economical *heat that money can buy.* QUIET MAY *provides luxurious heat - clean heat - safe heat - automatic heat, affording the greatest amount of desirable heat for the least amount of money. There is no fuel to handle - no by-products to remove, no fires to bank, no drafts to adjust - any temperature desired for absolute comfort is at your command. You can control the temperature of your entire house, simply by setting the thermostat which can be done with one finger.*

The Ol' Baby Touching the Thermostat trick! This system is so simple even a toddler can make it work.

QUIET MAY dependability *relieves you of all responsibility in the matter of heating your home. You may go away for a day, a week or even a month and find perfect comfort when you return. Let's take a trip though the following pages and see the reasons for QUIET MAY's* dependable superiority.

In other words, your pipes won't freeze and flood your house.

Now, I'm going to show you just the first page of the technical section of this booklet. Notice how the writer "talks on paper," using word pictures to explain the somewhat complicated engineering principles involved in the workings of this burner.

It's beautifully done, isn't it?

Gerotor—"The heart that won't wear out!"

An Exclusive
QUIET MAY *Feature*

THE GEROTOR PUMP

The heart of the QUIET MAY is the Gerotor Pump. It is an exclusive QUIET MAY patented feature and is not found in *any* other oil burner equipment.

There are *no* gaskets, *no* packing. A Gerotor Pump is practically leak-proof.

The scientific principle underlying the Gerotor Pump has been known for 147 years, but it remained for QUIET MAY engineers, a great inventor and a wizard in mechanical production to translate the scientifically correct principle into a practical reality.

If you understand the "law of relativity"---if you know your "indeterminate equations"---if the intricacies of calculus are as familiar to you as simple addition---then you can grasp the principle underlying Gerotor, otherwise, your interest will probably follow what Gerotor *does* rather than why or how it does it. In fact Gerotor, made possible through the solution of a labyrinth of kinetic problems, is the embodiment of simplicity itself.

"Gerotor" has a two-fold function. It draws the fuel oil from the storage tank to the burner and then develops the necessary pressure to atomize the fuel oil for correct combustion. It performs its work noiselessly, uniformly and economically.

Tests have been conducted wherein Gerotor Pumps have operated over 713,340,000 revolutions with no detectable wear. The liquids used in the tests ranged from the lightest to the heaviest fuel oils. Pump wear previously experienced with heavy, yet less expensive oils, has been entirely eliminated. Imagine the conventional pump with the impact and wear of two gears rotating in opposite direction as against the smooth rolling contact of Gerotor---two gears or rotors revolving in the same direction.

So fine is its precision manufacture and so efficient its operation that the power required to drive Gerotor is much less than that used by other pumping systems. This means a saving in electrical consumption and insures minimum operating cost.

Gerotor is simple, sturdy, powerful, resistant to wear, and economical to operate.

Gerotor's reserve pumping power may be likened to that of the heart of a centenarian. "Gerotor" is "The Heart That Won't Wear Out." It is "Built to Last a Lifetime."

Coming of Age

Advertising didn't get to be as good as the May Oil Burner Company's all by itself. The industry learned as it grew. Back in those days, people knew what they wanted. The world was ripe with invention and promises of greater comfort and convenience. Hydronic heating systems were new and anyone who'd seen one wanted one.

But industry advertising at the turn of the century meant nothing more than keeping your name before the public's eye. It was a classic case of "If you build it, they will come" - as long as you were willing to wait long enough.

I have a 1904 copy of *Domestic Engineering* magazine. On page four there's an ad that asks the reader, *"Have you noticed how many inquiries you have received lately for prices on Wilks heaters? You would better send for our new catalogue and discounts so as to be prepared to quote prices."*

That's the entire ad. The people at Wilks just sat back and waited for the mail. They made no mention of *why* you should buy a Wilks heater. They didn't distinguish their heater from the other guy's heater. They just waited for building owners to ask contractors about their product.

Maybe that's why you don't see too many Wilks heaters anymore.

Salesmanship In Print

In the heating industry, advertising has always reflected the times. It's ebbed and flowed with the state of the economy and it has changed its philosophy over the years.

If you compare the old ads to the new, an interesting story emerges.

Over the past 70 years or so, manufacturers have shifted their focus from the end user to the contractor. They began by teaching the contractor about their product. They told him what their product was, how it worked, where it went and why he needed it. And then they showed him how to sell it.

Nowadays, most of the ads assume the contractor knows all these things. The trouble is, many contractors don't, especially when it comes to hydronics.

I recently spoke with an advertising guy who works for a major manufacturer of hydronic heating equipment. We were talking about a simple off-the-shelf product they'd been selling since the 1930s. This item was like sugar in a grocery store as far as they were concerned.

"You know what? The average contractor doesn't know what this thing does," I said.

"I find that impossible to believe!" the ad man shot back. "We've been selling these for years. *Everyone* knows what it does. We'd be wasting our time and valuable advertising space by telling the contractor what it *does*. They already use them. Our job is to get them to use *ours* instead of our competitors."

"They use them, sure," I said, "but they really don't know why they're using them. They're buying out of habit."

"You're nuts."

"How are your sales?" I asked.

"Sales are off. But that's because of the recession."

"Are you sure?" I asked, "Maybe you're selling less because the contractor either forgot or never really learned, why he buys your products."

"Nah, you're wrong," the ad man said. "*Everyone* knows. Look at how long we've been making them!"

You know what the ad man forgot? He's selling to a parade. Contractors just keep passing by. Some have never heard his story because he hasn't told it in years. And if the contractor doesn't know the story, he certainly can't pass it on to the consumer.

One of the greatest shifts in advertising took place in the early 1920s when Claude C. Hopkins wrote a little book called *Scientific Advertising.* This book changed the manufacturing world in a big way because it redefined advertising as "Salesmanship In Print."

Mr. Hopkins wrote, "Remember that the people you address are selfish, as we all are. The best ads ask no one to buy. They're based entirely on service. They offer wanted information. They cite advantages to users."

In other words, a good ad is salesmanship in print. It answers the question, What's in it for me?

The heating industry took Hopkins seriously (as did most smart marketers of the time). Almost immediately, the ads in the trade journals and consumer magazines shifted toward what the product *does* and away from simply mentioning "you would better send for your catalogue." In the heating industry, the ads focused on comfort as the main benefit of the product. They taught the contractor how to sell the product by concentrating more on benefits than on features. The philosophy was, "No one ever bought a drill because they wanted to own a drill. They bought a drill because they wanted to own a *hole*."

Selling Holes

Consider this excerpt from a 1921 ad for the Moline steam heating system.

> *"Did you ever try submitting a proposal on Moline Heat, Mr. Contractor? Thousands of you have done so, we know, and this advertisement is not directed to those who have had the satisfaction time and again of having their proposals on Moline Heat accepted - but to you who have not tried."*

Notice how they immediately try to establish a partnering arrangement with the contractor. They're there to help him make money. And then they begin to lay out their case,

> *"Are you still submitting proposals on the old methods of heating, ordinary steam systems that use leaky, sputtering air vents on radiators - or hot water systems with large, cumbersome pipes and radiators, and that are slow to respond? Or on systems that use automatic or thermostatic traps or other 'jiggers' on the return ends of radiators and coils? If you are, well, you are going to change your mind some day - and you might as well do it now."*

Notice how they put a subtle emphasis on the end user's comfort. This was key in the old ads. The manufacturers showed the contractor how to build his business by avoiding problems and by providing his customer with comfort. Listen:

"With Moline Heat, no vacuum pumps are necessary to maintain circulation, no traps or any other get-out-of-order devices are necessary at the return end of the radiators - yet Moline Heat circulates steam through every radiator at a few ounces of pressure, no matter how large the job."

And then they get down to the real nitty-gritty, the thing that most interests the contractor:

"There is nothing that means so much to your business as profit. We know that - and so do you. Still, profit depends upon the satisfaction you give your customers. That is a fact that has been absolutely established. You cannot continue to satisfy your customers with old, antiquated methods - that's another fact."

They never directly ask for an order. They end, instead, with an offer:

"When you figure your next job for a factory, school, apartment, residence, or any other building, send us a set of the building plans, and then submit your proposal on Moline Heat and see what happens."

Partnering. And a focus on the entire system - how it works and what it offers the end user. These were the two driving forces behind the ads in the early days of the heating industry. They reflected an attitude that was widespread, one which continued right up until World War II.

I'm looking at a 1941 Bell & Gossett ad for what they called their "Triple-Duty Monoflo System." The equipment, installed on a boiler, dominates the page, but my attention is drawn to a series of small photos that surround the boiler. The photos feature a smiling family.

The first shows a mother, father and two children sitting at a breakfast table. The caption reads, "No early morning chills. Forced circulation speeds heat to every radiator in a moment's time." (A solid benefit, right?)

The second finds mother at the sink, washing the dishes. "Plenty of hot water. The B&G heater supplies an ample quantity - winter and summer." (Another benefit.)

We move down to a photo of an infant sitting in a washtub. "No chills or drafts. Radiant sun-like heat from the radiators keeps the temperature uniform." (A baby benefit!)

Then mom and dad with another couple. They're playing cards. The caption states, "Solid comfort late at night. Monoflo Heating is on the job every hour." (A benefit that will impress the neighbors.)

And finally, the happy couple, smiling as they sit with their family-budget book. "...And at the end of the month, fuel bills prove that Monoflo Heating is amazingly economical." (A tremendous benefit to this end-user family.)

Now keep in mind this ad was aimed at contractors, not homeowners. Bell & Gossett was following the common practice at the time *of showing the contractor how to sell their product to the end user by focusing on benefits.* Or put another way, they concentrated more on what the product *did* than what the product *was*. They didn't assume the contractor knew what their products did and what benefits the products offered the home owner. They sold the holes.

So When Did The Parade Stop?

We had this suburban building boom following World War II and with it came a change in advertising focus among the manufacturers of hydronic heating equipment. There was a subtle shift toward *features* and away from benefits. It was as though the manufacturers decided that everyone now knew how these products worked and were well versed in how to sell them.

Consider this excerpt from a 1952 Bell & Gossett ad:

"The B&G Booster is the basic unit of a B&G Hydro-Flo Forced Hot Water Heating System. It is built as a horizontally driven unit for sound engineering reasons which have demonstrated their practical value in thousands of installations. This construction makes possible many desirable, exclusive features. For example, the patented water-tight seal eliminates a stuffing box."

And so on. See the way they began to stress features over benefits? What happened to the baby in the washtub and the "radiant sun-like heat?" What happened to the benefits?

The industry, it seems, had come to a point where manufacturers believed the parade had stopped marching. They assumed contractors knew all about their products and were now more than capable of selling them to the end user with no help whatsoever.

Business was booming and the days of competition had begun. But somewhere along the way we somehow lost track of the words of Claude C. Hopkins: *"The best ads ask no one to buy. They're based entirely on service. They offer wanted information. They cite advantages to users."*

Today, when you open most any trade publication you'll find ads that focus almost entirely on features, and give very little time to end-user benefits. Some of these ads address neither. For example, Taco, Inc. recently built an ad around this statement:

> *"Saying 'a pump is a pump' is like saying 'football is football.' It's never safe to assume everyone is talking about the same thing. Take Taco's '00' Series, including our '007' workhorse. They're the only water-lubricated circulators designed and built right here in America, specifically developed for American hydronic heating system."*

Meanwhile, at my hydronic heating seminars, contractors constantly ask these questions: "Dan, can you explain how a circulator works and why I always see them on the return side of the system? Do they work on the other side as well? How do I size a circulator? How can I tell if I need a bigger one?"

These are the questions the ads answered in the old days. Those ads offered wanted information and they cited advantages to the end users. Rarely do we see this information offered nowadays. And yet, these are the questions contractors ask. If contractors don't know these things, how can they possibly have success when they try to explain these things to the end user?

So who reaches the end-user? This is where things get *really* interesting. The people who have jumped into the breech in recent years are the giant home centers. The Home Depot and their ilk advertise directly to the end user, and if you look closely at their ads you'll notice several things:

- They remember that people are selfish, as we all are.

- They offer service.

- They offer wanted information.

- They cite advantages to the user.

- They ask no one to buy.

In other words, they've resurrected Claude C. Hopkins' ideas, and they're making a fortune with them. Wet Head marketers recognize this, and they make it work to their advantage. Wet Heads know who their customers are, and they know how to approach those customers.

4

Who Is *Your* Customer?

Before you can sell to them, you have to figure out who they are. That sounds silly, I know, but hear me out for a few minutes and I think it should make more sense.

Let's suppose you have a four-year-old daughter and an 18-year-old son. You want them both to do something, say, clean their rooms. At this point, they are your customers because you're trying to get them to do something that will be good for both of you.

Now, would you talk to your daughter the same way you would talk to your son? Probably not, right? With your daughter, you might make cleaning the room a game. You might offer to take her to McDonald's if she did a good job. You might give her a hug and tell her how important a clean room is to her. She'll be able to find her things when her friends come over to play.

Now what should you do about your 18-year-old son? Let's see, you might threaten to throw all his stuff out the window if he doesn't clean the room. My father once did that to me. Made a hell of an impression.

Different customers, different strategies. See what I mean?

Speaking of McDonald's, have you noticed how after years of peddling Happy Meals to little kids they're now selling Arch Deluxes to grown-ups? Read the business pages of your newspaper and you'll learn that McDonald's is redefining themselves by redefining their customers. A burger is <u>not</u> a burger.

You can learn a lot by watching how McDonald's goes about their business. They're very good at what they do because they spend a lot of time thinking about who their customers are.

I had about 100 people in a seminar once - a really mixed group that contained contractors, wholesalers, engineers and manufacturers, a whole cross-section of the hydronic heating industry.

I asked the manufacturers who they thought their customers were. Without hesitation, they said, "The wholesalers."

I asked the wholesaler the same question and to a man (and woman) they said, "Contractors!"

I then asked the contractors and they said, "Home owners."

The engineers? Well, I didn't ask the engineers because I was afraid they'd start drawing diagrams.

Now watch this. The manufacturers advertise to the contractors, and *not* to the wholesaler, whom they claim are their customers. How come? Because manufacturers figure wholesalers won't buy squat from them unless contractors ask for it first.

Interesting, isn't it?

It also turns out the wholesalers aren't advertising to the contractors. Instead, the wholesalers are advertising to the contractors' customers - the home owners! "Gotta compete with Home Depot!" they said.

Interesting. The contractors were the only group that advertised to the people they claimed were their customers - home owners - but they generally did such a crummy job of advertising that the home owners went to Home Depot anyway.

Which is why it's pretty important to get your thinking and your marketing program straight.

Who are *your* customers? And are you getting through to them? Maybe you'll target the high-end new construction market. Or maybe you'll specialize in the renovation of older homes. How about a specialty in warm floors? You might even decide to become a steam-heating expert. I met a guy in New England who did just that. He changed the name of his company and hired a freelance graphics artist to put together some turn-of-the-century letterheads, business cards and ads. He ran his ads in the PENNYSAVER that was delivered to an area where there were older homes. In his ad, he explained that he was a specialist in the lost art of steam heating. He promised that he could get rid of the knocking pipes, the spitting air vents, the high fuel bills, the unbalanced comfort in older homes.

His phone rang day and night.

And he had no competitors.

Look in your local PENNYSAVER and *Yellow Pages*. You see anyone doing this sort of work in your neighborhood?

That's what I mean about deciding who your customers are.

Now What Do Your Customers Really Want?

Once you've figured out who your customers are, take a moment to list the three things that are most important to them. Give this some thought before you write anything down. And if you don't know what's important to them, you should take a few days off to figure it out.

1.

2.

3.

Now that you've written these things down, take a hard look at your company. Are these the things you're offering your customers? And if not, why not? Be brutally honest with yourself.

Next, I'd like you to list the three biggest problems your customers are having.

1.

2.

3.

Are you offering solutions to these problems? And if you are, how are you letting your customers know that you have that solution?

If they don't know you can help, they're not going to call, right?

Why Should I Buy From You?

Okay, now I'd like you to list the top three reasons why I, as a potential customer, should buy from <u>you</u> and not from your competitor?

This is perhaps the most important thing you'll do today, so take your time.

1.

2.

3.

How did you do?

Are you doing a good job of making this distinction between yourself and the other guy? Are the reasons you're giving me in my self-interest. Are they good enough to make me want to deal with you? If they're not, you *really* should come up with some new ones, don't you think?

I once asked a young salesman from a boiler company this question. "I'm a home owner," I said. "Why should I buy *your* boiler and not the other guys?"

"Because our boiler has cast-iron push nipples," he said without hesitation.

"What's a push nipple?" I asked, just as a home owner might.

"Uh, it's the part of the boiler that holds the sections together," he said.

"What's a section?"

"It's a . . ." he started to gesture with his hands. "It's a part of the boiler that has the water in it. A boiler might have a lot of sections, you know?"

"I'm not sure I understand. Does your competitor's boiler also have sections?"

"Of course they do," he said, getting flustered. "All cast-iron boilers have sections."

"But only your boiler has cast-iron push nipples between the sections," I pressed on.

"No, other boilers have cast-iron push nipples, too, but the competitor you mentioned has rubber gaskets instead of push nipples."

"And that's bad?" I asked.

"Rubber gaskets can leak," he said.

"Do cast-iron push nipples ever leak?" I asked.

"Not as much as gaskets,"

"Do furnaces leak?" I asked.

"Uh, no."

"Maybe I should buy a furnace then. Furnaces are cheaper, aren't they?"

"Yeah, but you don't want a furnace."

"Why not?"

He waited a minute, and then he started to laugh. "Because I'm selling *boilers*," he said.

Really makes you want to buy one, doesn't it?

How Home-Owner Excitement Gets Diluted

Sixteen-million people watch the TV show, *This Old House*. They see Steve and Norm ripping down and building up, and the see Richard Trethewey installing these fine hydronic radiant floor heating systems. They get really interested in this and they call their local plumber. Most of the time, the plumber will tell the home owner that radiant floor heating is too expensive. The plumber says this because he doesn't know how to size or install hydronic radiant heating equipment. He'll try his best to talk the home owner into buying a system he knows something about. He'll tell the home owner that hydronic radiant heating is no good, that it leaks, that it can't possibly work, that no one will ever be able to service it.

More often than not, the story ends here because the plumber has had so much practice losing potential business. He's *really* good at losing business, and he's *very* persuasive.

If the home owner is persistent, the plumber will tell him to call someone else because he, the plumber, doesn't want to be responsible for the bad things that will probably happen. The home owner takes his advice and calls another plumber. He gets the same answer, so he tries a third and is told the same thing.

Now, all of this bothers the home owner because Richard Trethewey seems to know what he's doing. If this stuff didn't work, it probably wouldn't be on national television where 16 million people could see it. He decides to do some research of his own.

He gets in his car and drives down to his local plumbing & heating supply house. The guy at the counter tells him they only sell wholesale, but he does give him the 800 phone numbers of a few radiant tubing manufacturers. Then he goes about the business of waiting on the contractors - *real* customers.

The home owner drives back to his house and calls the manufacturers. He gets to speak to nice people who promise to send more literature. Sure enough, it arrives a few weeks later. The home owner looks at the literature, which is written for contractors. He gets a bit confused, but he's still as interested in hydronic radiant heating as he was in the beginning. Maybe even more so. He looks on the back of the manufacturers literature and sees the name of the local rep. He calls the rep, and gets to speak to more nice people. They explain that they sell only to wholesalers, but that they'd be happy to send some product literature. He explains that he already has enough literature to start his own company, and that he would now like to buy something. He tells them about Trethewey and all, and they tell him that the stuff Trethewey is showing is not the stuff they sell. He says he really doesn't care at this point, and could they recommend a contractor in his area who would be willing to take his money. The rep doesn't want to show favoritism so he recommends at least three contractors.

The home owner calls the contractors, and they all show up at his house. Each comes up with a different way to do the job, and they each accuse the other of being an idiot with a long list of failed jobs and lawsuits.

This confuses the customer so much that he decides to forget the whole business.

With 16 million people watching Trethewey on *This Old House*, as well as all those other home owner shows, a smart Wet Head will find a way to get noticed *directly* by the home owner.

Here's why. The chain of distribution is the same as it has always been - manufacturer to manufacturers rep to wholesaler to contractor to end user - *but for the first time*, and because of TV, much of the excitement over hydronic heating is coming from the bottom up instead of the other way around.

Home owners are interested in hydronics, especially radiant hydronics, but they're having a hard time spending their money because most contractors haven't recognized this shift in the direction of excitement. Manufacturers are getting calls from home owners but manufacturers aren't set up to handle home owners. They send these referrals through their traditional chain of distribution, and the excitement gets diluted along the way

Smart Wet Heads recognize this and make themselves noticeable to the home owners. Smart Wet Heads know how to pay attention. They look at the world around them - and they learn from it.

5

Paying Attention

If you're like me, you probably have an old pair of boat shoes you've been wearing for years. They're like old friends, and they just seem to get more comfortable with age, don't they?

Now, if you were in the business of selling boat shoes you'd have to figure that people are not going to be buying from you that often. You may see that shoe customer once every five years or so. A good pair of boat shoes can last that long - and longer!

The point being, you don't get to tell your story as often as you might like to that customer. He may buy boat shoes about as often as he buys heating equipment.

Which is why you should pay attention to the way different companies sell their boat shoes.

I have a Sears catalog on my desk and it's open to page 328 where the boat shoes are. Here's how Sears describes their shoes:

This may be the most comfortable boat shoe you'll ever wear. Genuine leather uppers and sock linings, together with the "Luxury Liner" lightweight footbed make it feel and look great. Skid resistant synthetic rubber sole. Genuine handsewn moccasin construction with rawhide laces. Price: $66.00

Sounds pretty good, doesn't it? They included all that "Luxury Liner" and lightweight footbed stuff. They also imply that you won't go skidding off the deck, should you decide to wear your new boat shoes on a boat. Sears does a credible job of selling shoes.

And then there's L.L.Bean. Listen:

Our most popular moccasins since the 1920s. Made from highest-quality top-grain leather. Handsewn with true moc construction so leather completely wraps and forms to your foot for a custom fit. Padded insole is removable, allowing wear with heavier-weight socks. ¾-length leather sock liner ensures years of wear with our without insole. Rubber outsole with full-length foam core for a cushioned step. Made in Maine. Price: $69.00

Not bad, eh? Notice how L.L.Bean takes the time to explain what moccasin construction is? Sears just tells you they use "genuine handsewn moccasin construction with rawhide laces," but Bean gives you the details. "It wraps around your foot for a more custom fit."

Bean gives a benefit where Sears gives a feature. See the difference?

But now let's listen to how a master marketer tells their story.

I have a Lands End catalog on my desk. On page 41 they show a pair of boat shoes that look just like the ones in the Sears and the L.L.Bean catalogs.

Listen to the wonderful way Lands End describes their shoes.

We got together with one of Maine's premier marine shoemakers, specialists in handsewn boating shoes since 1948. Then <u>we</u> added a few things all our own.

Our leather is a densely oiled nubuck, a "mechanical" leather developed for use in the high-pressure seals on oil-pumping equipment. This "industrial strength" density is also just the stuff for superior marine leather. Wets up slower, dries out quicker, and remains soft when it dries.

Then there's our exclusive performance outsole. Molded from two different densities of rubber. A rigid white rubber frame for stability and support, a softer honey-colored thread for grip.

Where your shoe meets the wet deck, there's a high-tech channeled bottom, designed for slip-resistance forward-backward <u>and</u> side-to-side - across the entire surface of the tread!

Despite the "techy" additions, we've stuck pretty close to the handsewn boat moc that's become so traditional. After all, you'll still be wanting something to look good with your flannels. Made in USA.

All around the photograph of the shoe, which looks *exactly* like the shoe in the Sears and L.L.Bean catalogs, Lands End adds these notes.

- *Mesh drain holes in non-corroding brass keep water from "pooling up" inside.*

- *Functional collar lace let's you snug the fit up all around, so heels won't slip out.*

- *Handsewn moccasin upper wraps completely under foot. Waxed cotton thread won't stretch when wet.*

- *Outsole is lock-stitched to moccasin bottom.*

Lands End charges $85 for their shoes; Sears and L.L.Bean charge $66 and $69, respectively.

Which shoes would you buy?

People will *always* be willing to pay more if you can convince them they are *getting* more.

Lands End proves this every day.

This is the approach you should take with every proposal you write. Spend time thinking about what makes you different from your competition. Are you faster? Cleaner? More technically competent? More courteous? Do you install systems that deliver more creature comfort? (If you're a Wet Head you certainly do!)

Spend time thinking about how you can get your message across to your potential customers. Speak to them in plain-English, just as Lands End does. Find the features that set you apart, but explain only the *benefits* those features will bring to the customer.

Features Are Nice, But People Buy Benefits

I found two advertisements in a consumer magazine. The first is from Heatway, the hydronic radiant tubing supplier. The headline reads,

Warm Every Foot in the House.
Every square foot. Every bare foot.

There's a photo of a barefoot man reaching down to touch the warm floor. You can see the tubing through the floor.

Here's what the ad has to say.

Feet love to walk on a radiant floor. There's no match for comfort or efficiency. Today's technology enables heating of even the largest homes. A Heatway system will warm either slab or elevated floors underneath hardwoods, tile, marble or carpeting. It will also snowmelt a walk or driveway with ease. Whether you're building a new house or remodeling, you can trust Heatway's UL-listed products. For free design assistance or answers to your questions, give us a call today. Every foot in the house will thank you.

Contrast this with the following ad from Thermal Ease, another hydronic radiant tubing supplier. Same magazine. The headline reads,

The Switch to PEX Pipe Is On!

And here's what they have to say.

Thermal Ease PEX is now NSF listed. HEATING/ POTABLE WATER USES. Manufactured to: CSA B 137.5 ASTM F877 in our ISO 9002 certified plant. Call for a catalog of our competitively priced potable and radiant heating systems.

Now you're a home owner, right? Heatway is selling warm feet. Thermal Ease is selling code approvals. Who you gonna call?

In the same magazine you can find an ad from GlowCore, the high-efficiency boiler manufacturer. They show a drawing of a boiler backed up by a graphic of hydronic radiant tubing laid under a floor. The headline reads,

GlowCore High Efficiency Heating
GB Series "A" Gas Boiler
The Radiant Floor Boiler

I suppose that's a good start. They're letting the home owner know their boiler is made specifically for radiant floors and that it's efficient. But then GlowCore leaves the home owner all alone with this information.

- *92% AFUE*

- *Direct Vent*

- *Sealed Combustion*

- *Compact Cabinet*

- *Low NOX*

- *Low Mass*

- *Low Temp.*

- *Shock Proof*

- *No Minimum Water Temperature*

That's it, there are no other words on the page, other than their address and phone number. Now, you're a home owner. Did you get any of this? What's GlowCore talking about? They spent money on this ad, and then they left you all alone by yourself to figure it all out.

Maybe if you were a contractor you'd get the significance of these features. Maybe. Maybe not.

Suppose GlowCore had spent their money talking benefits instead of features. For instance.

- Chimneys take up valuable living space, so we did away with them!

- Our boiler is *so* small you won't even know it's there.

- With our boiler, you'll get more comfort for every dollar you spend on fuel. Try as you might, you wont find a boiler that costs less to operate from year to year.

- Our boiler doesn't pollute the air you and your children breathe.

- We designed our boiler *specifically* for modern radiant heating systems.

Better? I didn't take up any more space than they did.

Here's why GlowCore needs to take a close look at that ad. In the same magazine you'll an ad from Burnham, another boiler manufacturer, and GlowCore's competitor. Burnham's headline reads,

Wrap your family in comfort.

That's a pretty good start, isn't it? Family, comfort, security. I'm listening already.

And here's what Burnham has to say.

Your family's health and comfort deserve only the best heating options. So write now for your FREE "Home Heating Ideas" booklet. You'll also get a list of local America's Home Heating Team contractors who can specify a reliable Burnham boiler that's right for your home.

Not many words, but some solid benefits: Health and comfort. Free home-heating ideas. A list of qualified contractors. Design services. These are things that grab a home owner's interest. If you were leafing through that magazine, looking for a new boiler, which ad would grab your attention? Who would you call?

Another magazine contained an ad from tekmar, the Canadian controls manufacturer. The headline reads,

We Have The Answer . . .

The ad shows a picture of a tekmar control along with a schematic of a "typical heating system." They follow by listing these product features:

- *Microprocessor based PI control with LCD display*

- *Two boiler or one boiler and one pump outdoor reset application*

- *Warm weather shut down (WWSD)*

- *Programmable settings*

- *Minimum boiler supply temperature*

- *Sensor error messages*

Any idea what these features mean to you? Could you explain them to a home owner? Where are the benefits? Should tekmar assume you understand these features?

Here's another ad, this one from Heat-Timer, another controls manufacturer.

The headline reads,

New From Heat-Timer.
Indoor/Outdoor Reset Controls for Hydronic and Radiant Heating Systems.

Here's their message.

The Heat-Trol Value Series establishes a building's ambient comfort by varying the temperature of the circulating heating water in response to changes in the outdoor temperature. This control method, known as Hot Water Reset, can be accomplished in a variety of ways. By direct operation of a single on/off, lo/hi, or full modulating boiler staging multiple boilers or through modulation of 2, 3, and 4 way motorized valves.

You got that? They then list these features:

- *Adjustable Reset Ratios*

- *Adjustable Offset*

- *Adjustable Outdoor Cutoff*

- *Adjustable Setback*

- *Adjustable Morning Boost*

- *Adjustable Operating Differential (HWM-100 Only)*

- *Adjustable Minimum Water Temperature Setpoint (HWM-100, 300 & 500)*

- *Domestic Hot Water Priority Mode (HQM-100 Only)*

- *Adjustable Reaction Time (HWM-500 Only)*

- *Adjustable Maximum Water Temperature Set Point (HWM-200 & 300)*

- *Adjustable Burner Ignition Point*

- *Manual Override*

- *Remote Override Capability*

- *LED Indication*

- *Automatic Rotation of Lead Stage.*

But what do these features mean to *you*? And how many of these could you explain if your customer asked. Where are the benefits? The engineers at the factory may have grown up with these features. I'm sure they know them inside and out, but will the customer get the message? And if the customer doesn't get the message, what's the point of the ad?

Fuelish Advertising

I grew up on Long Island thinking everyone in the world heated with oil. That's understandable, I suppose, because on Long Island we have more people heating with oil than anywhere else in the country.

As I said, there used to be hundreds of Mom-and-Pop oil companies, but these have been gobbled up by larger retail dealers. We're now left with much bigger companies that have the budgets to advertise their product and their services in the newspaper. These guys compete with each other and with the gas utility.

How do these big oil companies tell their story? Do they focus on product benefits? I have an ad from a local oil company on my desk. Here's the headline.

Next to any hot deal we're . . . Cheaper! Better! Faster!

I once wrote a little book called *The Golden Rules of Hydronic Heating.* One of the Golden Rules was, "You can have it good. You can have it fast. You can have it cheap. Pick two." This particular oil company, however, can give you all three - good, fast *and* cheap. Imagine that.

This same company once ran another ad with the headline,

We're the Below-Cost Leaders,
and We Will Beat Any Other Dealer's Price
By At Least $50.
What Else Is There To Say?

They focus on the consumer's sense of selfishness, sure, but they neglect those wonderful intangibles that the people who made the Quiet May oil burner once trumpeted - health, cleanliness, leisure time, family togetherness, peace of mind, love, and friendship.

They focus instead on Cheaper! Better! Faster! Is this progress?

Break-Downs

Oil heat has been popular around here for so many years that its popularity now often works *against* the oil companies. The gas utility runs ads stressing that oil heat is "old technology" and in need of constant service because most of the systems *are* so old. But that's what happens when you're popular, right? You stick around and you get old.

Now the way some oil companies respond to this is just brilliant. They run photos of their service people. They get these guys, put them in their uniforms and stand them in front of their service trucks. They tell them to smile. They take their pictures, and they put them in the newspaper.

The headline reads something like, Hey, we have <u>lots</u> of service technicians!

The gas company turns around and says, "Now, those are the guys we were telling you about. See how old and outdated their equipment is? They need all these service technicians and all those service trucks just to keep that old junk running. Why don't you get something new? Like gas heat."

And the oil guy in the ad just stands there smiling like the village idiot.

Dirty, Nasty Systems?

Exxon had this oil tanker that ran aground in Alaska. You may have read about it. It was in all the papers. Ironically, a guy from Long Island, this Joseph Hazelwood, happened to be driving the boat at the time of the crash. I thought that was very appropriate.

Anyway, the oil gushed out of the beached tanker and killed all the wildlife it could find and trashed the shoreline from Alaska to Chile. This gave both Exxon and oil in general a *really* bad name.

And then there was this fellow who set fire to most of the oil wells in Kuwait while on his way back to his own country, that being Iraq. It took a while to put those fires out, and this also gave oil a bad name.

So when the gas utility on Long Island runs ads that say oil heat is dirty and nasty, home owners tend to believe them. They see the fluid in their oil tanks as being the same stuff that killed all those poor animals in Alaska and polluted the air in the Middle East and beyond.

"Oil's dirty by nature," the utilities say. "It clogs up your heating equipment."

Some oil companies respond to this challenge by running ads that say "We add detergent to our oil so that it won't clog your equipment."

"There!" the gas utilities say. "Didn't we tell you! It's dirty. They have to use detergent - just like you use when you wash your dirty, greasy clothes."

A brilliant strategy on the part of the oil companies, don't you think?

Your Tank Is Leaking!

As I mentioned earlier, we have a gazillion buried oil tanks here on Long Island, and most have been in the ground for nearly fifty years. These tanks are made of steel. We get our drinking water from an aquifer, which is right below those buried oil tanks. The gas utility runs ads that tell people these tanks are environmental time bombs, just waiting to go off.

"Get rid of the tank, and get rid of your oil company while you're at it," the ads say. "Convert to gas and you'll never have to worry about anything."

The oil companies respond by publishing photographs of homes that have recently been converted into holes by a natural gas explosion. The headline reads, "Gas. It's a booming business."

Clever, eh?

The smart oil companies offer deals on removing those buried tanks. Some do it for free if you agree to buy oil from them for so many years. They turn a problem into an opportunity. That's smart.

A Fuelish Ploy

I got a call from a home owner not long ago that filled me with wonder.

"The man from the gas company told me that if I switched from dirty oil to clean natural gas I could get rid of those ugly oil stains on my walls. Is that true?"

"You have oil stains on your walls?" I asked.

"Yes. I mean that's what the man from the gas company told me."

"Where exactly are these 'oil' stains," I asked.

"Right over the radiators. They're smeared all over the walls. Ugly black oil stains."

"That's not oil," I said. "That's dirt from the convection currents moving through the radiator."

"Huh?"

"Look," I said, backing up a bit, "when the radiator heats the air in the room, the air rises. That makes the air near the floor scoot across and enter the bottom of the radiator. It's like a Ferris wheel."

"Oh, I get it," he said.

"Good. Now, over the course of the year, any dirt that's on the floor will work its way into the radiator and rise with the hot air. I'm sure that's what you're seeing on the walls."

"It's not oil?"

"Nope," I said, "not oil."

"Then why did the man from the gas company say it was oil? Isn't natural gas cleaner than oil? Why do I have stains on my wall?"

I wondered why the people from the oil company hadn't educated this guy at any point during all the years they serviced his account. They were in that house at least once a year doing a tune-up. If he had known what was happening to him, he might have hired a couple of kids during the summer to dress in white coveralls and go out to vacuum radiators. You know, talk about cleanliness? That intangible thing the gas company happened to be selling.

It might have made a difference.

Why So Defensive?

I often wonder how the oil companies managed to get themselves into a position where they're on the defensive all the time. I wonder why they don't go back to doing what the Quiet May folks did so well in 1934. Why aren't the modern oil companies selling intangibles such as comfort, economy, convenience, and health? Why are they spending so much time focusing on Better! Faster! Cheaper!

It's a battle worth watching if you're a Wet Head. You can learn a lot about oil companies, gas utilities and marketing in general if you just pay attention.

The oil company's ads in the newspapers usually show a lot of equipment - oil burners, water heaters, boilers and furnaces. However, they never address the points Quiet May once did. They focus on features such as AFUE (Annual Fuel Utilization Efficiency, in case you didn't know) instead of benefits, like healthier babies. Most consumers don't know one piece of equipment from the next when they look at those ads.

I have an ad from the gas utility that has a photo of a smiling customer touching his thermostat. He says, "Ever since we switched to gas heat, I can keep my house warm for a lot less." Right away, I thought of the photo of the baby and the mother in the Quiet May ad.

A home owner once called me to ask about a banging radiator. I asked her what type of heating system she had. She told me to hang on while she checked. She returned a few moments later and said, "I have a Honeywell system."

The gas utility knows most home owners look no further than their thermostat because, nowadays, few heating companies can get home owners excited about this stuff. The gas utility puts a guy with a thermostat in their ad because they know that's what the home owners are thinking about. Thermostats. Comfort.

But the oil companies keep screaming, Better! Faster! Cheaper!

Makes you wonder, doesn't it?

Pay Attention To The Way Some Contractors Tell Their Stories

If you look up "Hydronic Heating Systems" in my *Yellow Pages* you will find a note that tells you to "See Fireplace Equip. - Whole. & Mfrs."

This is one of Long Island's great mysteries.

When you look up "Fireplace Equip. - Whole. & Mfgs." you will find just that - fireplace equipment wholesalers and manufacturers. There's nothing there for Wet Heads, but this doesn't bother me as much as you might think it would because most home owners don't know the term "hydronics" anyway. If they, by chance, hear the term "hydronics" mentioned quickly on some TV show such as *This Old House*, they probably go to the *Yellow Pages* and look for "*Hydraulic* Heating Systems."

Where they will find nothing.

If I were advertising hydronic heating in the *Yellow Pages* I would *definitely* list my stuff under *Hydraulic* Heating Equipment. That's where everybody's looking.

Look up "Radiant Heat Systems" in my *Yellow Pages* and you will find a note directing you to "Heating Contractors." When you get to "Heating Contractors," you will find a long list of companies specializing in furnaces.

One of these guys runs a tiny ad in my *Yellow Pages* that I think is brilliant. In the smallest space imaginable this guy manages to say the following:

- I can fix your broken heating system in hours - not days.

- I run a drug- and alcohol-free shop.

- We're a reliable company.

- All of our technicians receive the latest diagnostic training.

- We use flat-rate pricing, which means you'll never pay extra for labor or hard-to-find parts.

- We install only the highest efficiency systems, both new and replacement.

- We are specialists in indoor air quality (duct cleaning).

- Your satisfaction is guaranteed.

See all those benefits? Oh, how I wish this man was a Wet Head!

Right next to this guy's ad is another guy with an ad twice as large. He uses his space to say,

- He is a specialist in gas and oil burners.

- He sells, installs, and services all brands.

- He's open 24 hours a day.

- He does residential, commercial and industrial work.

- He replaces steam pipes (which means he's a Wet Head).

You're a home owner, and you're looking at those two ads. You don't have the slightest idea what sort of heating system you have. All you know is what fuel you burn and who made your thermostat.

Which guy are you likely to call?

See the difference a strong, benefit-driven ad can make?

And by the way, out of the 154 heating contractors advertising in my *Yellow Pages*, not one of them claims to do radiant heating - hydronic or otherwise.

Why do we make it so hard for people to spend their money?

People watch the TV show, *This Old House* and they see Richard Trethewey loping around like a big happy Wet Head, installing all this hydronic radiant tubing, high-tech boilers, and whatnot. The home owner opens my *Yellow Pages*, desperately looking for someone to whom he might give his money, but what does he find?

He finds one-hundred-fifty-four contractors who do everything but *hydronic* radiant heat.

What an enormous opportunity there is for a Wet Head who is paying attention and who makes himself different from other contractors. Wet Head marketers are *always* doing things that are different.

6

Dare To Be Different

Every Saturday morning a guy drives by my house and hurls a plastic bag like a hand grenade over the top of his car toward my driveway. This bag contains all the week's circulars along with the *PENNYSAVER*, a small, newsprint magazine filled with little ads for tiny and not-so-tiny companies. Here, you will also find every moonlighter on Long Island.

I wait for the *PENNYSAVER* each week because I want to see if the local heating professionals have gotten any better at marketing their services.

Here's a sample of what I found on the last Saturday in November when it was just 31 degrees outside. I'm going to call each one of them "Joe's Plumbing & Heating" because you can't tell them apart anyway.

Joe's Plumbing & Heating: Fast friendly service, expert repair, installation, leaks fixed, drains unclogged, licensed, insured, Visa, MasterCard. (his phone number)

This last Joe doesn't put a question mark at the end of his ad, so I can only assume that *he's* the one who is tired of high prices, poor workmanship, estimates. Makes you just want to grab for that phone and call him, doesn't it?

Seriously, how have these guys used their space to distinguish themselves? It's almost as though they read the other ads and decide to make themselves sound the same.

You're the home owner. Who do you call?

In the same issue of the *PENNYSAVER* there's an ad for a company called Cap-A-Radiator Shops. Sure, it's a different industry, but listen to what these folks have to say - and how well they say it.

What Is A Heater Core?

A heater core is basically a miniature radiator that provides the interior of your vehicle with heat. In addition to providing comfort in cold weather, it can also be considered a safety item when you need to use your defroster.

Most motorists have little or no idea of how their heater/defroster system works. If you are getting little or no heat from your car, there are many parts that may be the cause of the problem. A thermostat that is stuck open, faulty controls, low coolant level, stuck heater valve, air pockets or a clogged heater are just some of the common causes of poor heat.

Replacing parts until the problem is solved is not the way to fix your heater/defroster problem. Diagnosing the reasons for the problem is usually easy for a mechanic who has a lot of experience in automotive heater systems. Diagnosing a leaking heater core may be easy for anyone, but replacing a heater core can sometimes be a very time-consuming job and is best left to someone with a lot of experience. At Cap-A-Radiator we have the experience to handle your vehicle's heater problem, no matter how big or small.

Thank you,

Maria & Bill

(Their phone number)

Isn't that neat? They give you all this solid advice and free information. They even tell you their names. I like to think Maria & Bill have been happily married for years and would rather be down at the ol' Ca-p-A-Radiator Shop than anywhere else.

Don't you want to do business with these folks?

I'll bet Maria and Bill have a stack of Lands End catalogs in their magazine rack at home.

Now, to prove to you that you don't even have to be that great, you just have to pay attention, let's take Maria & Bill's ad and change just a few of the words.

We'll let one of the Joes use it in next week's *PENNYSAVER*.

What Is A Radiator?

A radiator is basically a device that provides the interior of your home with heat. In addition to providing comfort in cold weather, it can also be considered a safety device to keep your plumbing pipes from freezing during the winter.

Most home owners have little or no idea of how radiators work. If you are getting little or no heat from your existing system, there are many parts that may be the cause of the problem. A thermostat that is stuck, faulty controls, low water level, stuck valves, air pockets or a clogged boiler are just some of the common causes of poor heat.

Replacing parts until the problem is solved is not the way to fix your problem. Diagnosing the reasons for the problem is usually easy for a heating contractor who has a lot of experience in hydronic heating systems. Diagnosing a problem may be easy, but coming up with an innovative, money-saving, long-term solution is best left to someone with a lot of experience in hydronic heating. At Joe's Plumbing & Heating we have the experience to handle your home's heating problems, no matter how big or small.

Thank you,
Joe

(His phone number)

See? Nothing to it! If Maria and Bill can do it, so can Joe.

And so can you.

Imagine what would happen if you ran a short article such as this every week on a different subject. What is a radiant floor? What is a kick-space heater? What is a hydronic towel warmer? What is an outdoor reset control? What is PEX tubing? What is an indirect water heater?

Get the idea? Why, after a few weeks, I'll bet the first place readers turn will be to your ad, especially if you add some humor to it. People *love* humor. Here, listen.

It Stinks to High Heaven!

That's what Maria and Bill said when they asked us to remodel their bathroom. They have six sons, ranging in age from three to 13. They also had a small length of baseboard radiation right next to their old toilet.

"Those boys have never learned how to aim!" Maria complained. "As soon as the heat comes on, I can smell it. I wish we didn't have to go back to that same type of radiator."

"You don't!" I said, and then I explained about the wonders of radiant floor heating. "We can install some high-tech plastic tubing behind the new tile and run warm water through it," I explained. "I can tap right into your existing system and put all the controls inside your new vanity. It won't take up much space at all. It will give you warm floors and walls that are easy to keep clean instead of that old radiator."

"Didn't we see this on TV?" Bill asked.

"Probably. Everyone's talking about hydronic radiant heat nowadays. You'll save money on fuel too."

> That was last year. I stopped by Maria and Bill's the other day and they were really enjoying their warm, fresh-smelling bath. Maria gave me a big smile, "Now, can you make them pick up their dirty laundry?"
>
> I couldn't, but I'm sure I can solve your plumbing and heating problems. Call. We'll talk.
>
> Joe's Plumbing & Heating
>
> (His phone number)

You want to pull ahead of all those other Joes? Dare to be different.

Here's *How* to Be Different

A big part of successful marketing lies in the way you use words to describe what you have to offer. Think in terms of the customer's self-interest, and then use words that would appeal to those interests.

For instance, they just opened a new movie theater in the next town. Now, you have to understand that on Long Island we are not without movie theaters. If you throw a stick, you'll probably hit at least a half-dozen multiplex theaters. You could spend the rest of your life in Long Island movie theaters and never see the same film twice.

So when you open a new movie theater, how do you get people to go to your place instead of your competitor's.

You make yourself different!

To have a movie theater you need a few basic items: a screen, a projector, speakers, seats, darkness, a film to show, popcorn. That's it. Go to any movie and you know you're going to get this stuff.

Here's how the new movie theater in the next town makes themselves different.

They don't have just a screen and a projector. They have "Screens and projection systems that put you into the movie." Isn't that cool? They also claim, "Our cutting edge screens and projection systems will zap you into the action on screen."

Yikes! And they don't just have speakers they have, "Sound from another dimension. Fourteen luxurious cinemas with Multiplex Sound (Dolby/Digital), and Assistive Infra-Red Audio Equipment for the hearing impaired."

Go to most theaters and they give you a seat. Not the new theater in the next town. They give you "Comfort and luxury unknown to ordinary cinemas. Luxurious, deeply cushioned, reclining rocker seats with wide spacing between the rows."

They also have "Acres of well-lit parking lots." That's so you don't get mugged on your way out.

Now, given a wide choice, where would you want to go to the movies? Wouldn't you check out these new guys? Don't you want to be sitting in one of those luxurious, deeply cushioned, reclining rocker seats? Mmmmm!

Can you feel the power of words? All you have to do is think in terms of the customer's self interest, take the time to think about what makes you different, and then describe yourself in a delicious way.

Here's another one for you. Two of my kids wear contact lenses. They go to a doctor named Hart who is well known for contact lenses because he publishes a lot of articles in technical journals, which he then displays in his lobby. When you're sitting there waiting to see this guy you're forced to look at dozens of articles on the walls. They're written in a technical language no one in the lobby can understand, but I'll tell you, it makes you feel as though you're getting your money's worth. This guy is the best! You know why? He has all these articles on the walls!

Dr. Hart has to compete with places that do eyeglasses in a hour and contact lenses almost as quickly. These chain stores have huge budgets for advertising in the newspaper and on the radio and TV. These places are like Home Depots for eyeballs.

Dr. Hart has one office, and he can't possibly compete with these people on price. So what does he do? He plays off of what the big guys are doing to make his point.

The chain stores always offer a coupon. Clip in and bring it in for money off on your next pair of contacts. Dr. Hart publishes a coupon too when he advertises in the local *PENNYSAVER*. It catches your eye, as a coupon should, but here's how it reads.

The Coupon You *Don't* Want

The contact lens is a medical device. Improper or inadequate or unprofessional contact lens treatment can result in permanent eye damage. Often coupons make sense. But NOT for the selection of your contact lens doctor.

People read Dr. Hart's ad and they start thinking about their eyeballs. They look at the competitor's ad and then they make a decision.

You have to make an appointment with Dr. Hart weeks in advance, and then you're lucky if you get a seat in his lobby. He's doing *something* right.

Maybe you've run coupons in your ads before. Ten bucks off a service call, Senior Citizens Discount, whatever. I'd like you to use your imagination for a minute. What would you say in a *backwards* coupon like Dr. Hart's?

Maybe it would be something like this?

The Coupon You'll <u>Never</u> Use

This coupon entitles you to a free troubleshooting call on your new hydronic heating system.

(No one has ever actually *used* this coupon because our work is so good it doesn't require troubleshooting! We do it perfectly the *first* time, every time. You've made the <u>right</u> decision.)

Use your imagination. Watch the way people in other industries do things. Pay attention to the world around you, and borrow liberally.

What I Borrowed From Neiman Marcus

Neiman Marcus, the high-class Texas department store chain, sent us one of their glossy catalogs and I tore into it because I'm very interested in people who will consider buying things like His-and-Hers Lear jets. Neiman Marcus always features some wild and crazy thing like that in their catalog and it's no joke; they always wind up selling the thing.

What a country.

Anyway, I was looking for a way to make an ad for my book *Used Stories* stand out in *Contractor* magazine. I figured I could borrow an idea from Neiman Marcus and here's the ad we ran.

I had a graphics artist paint a water color of the Tahiti scene with the books and the beer, and we ran the ad in full color.

We sold a *lot* of books.

I'm still waiting for someone to take us up on the trip. Interested?

Use your imagination, and never be afraid to have fun. For instance, feel

Imagine!

For a mere $250,000...

...Dan Holohan and his wife, The Lovely Marianne, will fly you to Tahiti, buy you a cold beer, and take turns reading to you from Dan's 296-page book, *Used Stories*. This book is guaranteed to make you laugh, make you think, and make you smarter than ever about the business of hydronic heating.

Or if you prefer, you may buy just the book for an incredibly low $25.00 and read it to yourself. Get your own beer.

The choice is yours, but be forewarned that we'll only be accepting twelve (once a month) orders for the Tahiti trip during 1997. *So act now!*

Book only?
A mere $25.00
We pay the postage, of course
(Tahiti trip not included)

Call 1-800-853-8882
to order with your major credit card,
or send your check to:

Dan Holohan Assoc. Inc.
63 North Oakdale Avenue
Bethpage, NY 11714

ORDER BY FAX
24 HOURS A DAY:
1-516-579-3046.
All our books come with a 30-day,
money-back guarantee.

free to steal from me, as I have stolen from the wonderful people at Neiman Marcus:

Imagine!

For a mere $250,000 . . .

I will fly you to Tahiti, sit with you on the beach, and explain the reasons why the warmth of hydronic radiant floor heating feels so much like the warmth of a Tahitian beach. Or, if you prefer, I can install one of these incredible hydronic systems in your home for considerably less than a quarter-mil.

The choice is yours, but I promise the glorious warmth will be the same.

Let's talk!

Go get 'em, Wet Head

Maybe You Think You're Not Advertising

I received a letter from a contractor in Pennsylvania the other day. Here's what he had to say.

Hello Dan,

Please send me a copy of your latest book. I have all your other books and they're good reading. Someday I hope to attend one of your seminars. However, there are none in our location, at present, we are too busy which makes travel out of the question.

Our company does not advertise. Just recently, we removed our company signs from three of our vans because we cannot keep up with all the work that is coming our way.

It seems good old word-of-mouth advertising is the best. Also, our family is a third generation plumbing and heating company. We've been around since the turn of the century.

Again, keep up the good work. And please excuse the hand-written note. I'm too busy to type!

Lucky guy, right?

I think he's missing an important point, though. Word-of-mouth advertising *is* advertising. But it's advertising you don't get to control. It can work for you, as in this case, or against you. Every company gets word-of-mouth advertising to some degree, but whether you find out about it in time depends on whether you're paying attention.

Just because you don't run an ad in the *PENNYSAVER* or the *Yellow Pages* or have your name on the side of your vans doesn't mean you're not advertising. Every time you work in a customer's house, you're advertising. You're selling your company, and you're helping them decide whether they'll recommend you, or use you again next time.

If you delight them with your differences, they probably will.

Say what you mean !

7

Telling Your Story
to Regular Human Beings

You'd never hand someone an envelope and say, "Enclosed please find our quotation for your project," would you? So how come you feel compelled to speak that way when you're writing a letter or a proposal?

Do you feel the need to be official?

Do you think this is what people expect from you?

Suppose you just wrote, "Here's the quotation I promised when we got together to discuss your project." Isn't that what you'd say if you were face to face?

So how come you don't just say it that way? That's what regular human beings like to hear.

Talking on paper is pretty easy. You just sit down and write exactly what you'd say if the person was there. In 1976, a friend gave me a book titled *Say What You Mean* (Harper & Row: ISBN 06-011291-3) Rudolph Flesch wrote it, and he taught me how to write - again. He taught me how to talk on paper. How to use short sentences.

Like this one.

He taught me how to translate technical stuff into plain-English so regular human beings would get it.

Whatever success I've had as a writer, I trace back to my first reading of this book. If you'd like to become better at getting your message across to your customers and other regular human beings, I urge you to get a copy of this little book and read it. It's the sort of book that can change your life.

How to Write An Ad Regular Human Beings Will Read

There's a recipe that Wet Head marketers use to write ads or stories that will appeal to their customers. The recipe has four ingredients:

1. First, look for a problem and run toward it.

2. Next, focus on the problem, and what you have to offer as a solution.

3. Then, think in terms of regular human beings - how they live, how they speak, how they would describe the problem if they were speaking to a friend.

4. Finally, use your imagination, drawing on your own experience as a regular human being and then just "talk" on paper.

The first step (Look toward a problem and run toward it) is one we went over before. Some people just see problems; Wet Heads see the opportunity in problems. Many of these problems have at their core the lack of comfort in most homes. Why are the floors so cold? How come this room's so hot while that room's so cold? Why do I pay so much money for so little comfort? Why is this room so drafty? Things like that. Wet Heads have solutions to every one of these common problems.

The second step has you *focusing* on what you can offer as a solution. This is where you'll find yourself marketing to a niche, a smaller segment of your neighborhood. Remember that I guy I knew who specializes in steam heat in an area where there are lots of older homes? He runs a small ad that promises he can get rid of banging pipes, uneven heat, spitting air vents, high fuel bills, and other common steam-related problems. Other contractors run from these jobs; my guy *specializes* in them. He's *focused*.

If the problem is cold floors or high fuel bills, the niche is hydronic radiant heat,. This is another area many contractors won't touch because they're not sure what they're doing. Smart Wet Heads know all about warm floors.

Step three reminds you to think in terms of regular human beings. Here's where you need to focus on benefits rather than features. Think about what the equipment *does*, not what it *is*. Don't think like a technician in this step; think like a home owner. What would appeal to you if you were on the receiving end of your proposed solution. Don't use technical terms that will confuse regular human beings.

Finally, you use your imagination, drawing on your own experiences as a regular human being. I gave you an example earlier about why it's a good idea to have a radiantly heated bathroom if you have six boys using the toilet. That came right out of my imagination, but it's based on stories people have told me. I just put the two together and then told my story. You can do this too!

I also told you about the idea that came to me while sitting with my kids in Dr. Hart's office. He had a non-coupon, a clever twist that caught my attention, and will surely catch your customer's attention as well.

Once you get the idea, just talk on paper. By that, I mean use the same words you would use if the customer were right there in the room with you. You wouldn't say, "Enclosed please find," or any of these other highfalutin terms people feel forced to use. You'd say, "Boy! Do I have the cure for what's ailing you!"

A Technique For Producing Ideas

I've written more than 250 articles for 13 magazines since 1988. My editors expect me to mail them fresh material every month. Each article is about 3-1/2 typewritten pages.

Sometimes I feel as though I'm standing in the ocean. I get hit with a wave, and before I can catch my breath, there's another one right behind it. I can see them coming, but I still have to deal with each one.

When I was younger, I used to suffer from writer's block. That's the awful feeling you get when you sit down in front of a blank sheet of paper (or a blank computer screen) and wonder what to do next. I would sometimes stare for days, and wonder if I was going to be able to make a living as a writer.

In 1986 I stumbled on a technique that helped me overcome writer's block once and for all. I've used it every day since then. You can use the same technique to generate new ideas for your business. All you have to do is follow the same recipe that's worked for me for more than ten years.

I found the secret in two little books, which you won't even have to read; I'll sum them up for you right here.

The first book (the one I found in 1986) fits in the palm of my hand and is just 62 pages long. Despite its tiny size, this book contains a great deal of good advice. It's called *A Technique for Producing Ideas*, and it was written by James Webb Young in 1940.

James Webb Young was a giant in the advertising business. Late in his career, he was asked to present his thoughts to the graduate business students at the University of Chicago. This book is, essentially, that speech. His technique for producing ideas works. I use it daily, and I don't know what I'd do without it. It consists of five simple steps.

1. Gather raw material constantly. You're in Burger King and you consider what they print on their place mats. You're driving behind a U-Haul truck and you notice how they list the benefits of renting that truck right on the truck itself. You're walking through a Home Depot and you pay attention to the questions home owners ask the employees - and how the employees answer those questions. You're waiting on line at the supply house and you notice how manufacturers display their products. You're reading your junk mail and paying attention to the way they try to grab your attention before you can toss it in the garbage. You notice the copywriter's use of words. You note the colors they use on the mailing. You pay attention to what *catches* your attention.

I spend a lot of time waiting in airports. Since I make my living as a writer, I'm always on the prowl for people I can use in my stories. As I wait for my plane, I'll jot down some of the images I see, knowing that at some point I'll be able to introduce these folks to you.

For instance, here are a few images from a recent wait in Chicago's O'Hare airport.

His hair looked like the pasta special - a tangled, wet clump that sat heavy on the top of his flat head.

The bags beneath his eyes looked like overripened plums.

He stared at the Wall Street Journal *as though it was do-it-yourself instructions for a bunk bed.*

Her hair was the color of bran flakes.

You could have baked a personal pan pizza on either one of those earrings.

He pushed his belly ahead of him like it was a shopping cart with one loose wheel.

She stamped her cane on the ground as though she intended to plant a tulip bulb.

The big man squinted at the Departures board as though daring it to change.

He struggled ahead of the luggage as though it were a dull plow and the concourse a rocky field.

She carried a small cup of Starbucks coffee, and enough napkins to absorb Lake Michigan.

I've gathered hundreds of these images in a computer file. When I have to write a story, I'll read through them and begin to see regular human beings doing what they do. I'll let my imagination wander.

In another computer file, I keep the seeds of technical stories. These are things I've seen or heard about that at some point will work their way into an article or a book.

For instance:

Master float & thermostatic traps make steam distribution even worse because they allow the returns to pressurize.

Plumbers like to hang pipes straight. That doesn't work in a steam system.

Air trapped in the radiators adds to the expansion capacity of the system. This is especially true of free-standing, cast-iron radiators. When you vent the radiators you may find the relief valve pops because there's either not enough charge in the compression tank, or the tank is undersized.

The Dead Men used to hook up gravity hot water radiators bottom to bottom. The water would circulate slowly (by gravity) into the radiator sections. When you add a circulator, though, you make the water move through the radiator very quickly. That means you'll get less heat than you did before because the cold water in the top of the radiator won't fall toward the radiator's outlet. The hot water's already there. Throttle the inlet valve to slow the flow and you'll solve the problem. Want more heat? Throttle the valve? It doesn't make sense, but it works.

In a primary/secondary system, you have to account for all the water in the system when you're sizing the compression tank. If the tank is too small, it may work when some of the zones aren't calling. But on the coldest days of the year, when all the zones call for heat, the tank may not be large enough. The relief valve will pop. The same applies to a reset system. You have to size the tank based on the hottest water temperature the system will see. If you undersize the tank, the relief valve will pop - and always on the coldest days of the year.

I combine these technical sketches with the people sketches, and I imagine them both into a story. Then all I have to do is write down what I see in my mind's eye.

Anybody can do this. The secret is to keep those idea files full because if you search for an idea or a new solution to a business problem with nothing in front of you but a blank sheet of paper, you'll get stuck. I guarantee it.

But if you have a file, you can search through all those neat business ideas you've come across over the years. And as you browse through all those cool things you've seen other people do, things will begin to percolate in your brain.

That's when you do this:

2. Work the material over in your mind, looking for new combinations of old elements. Mix the pieces up like Scrabble tiles and see what you get. What if U-Haul had place mats? What if Burger King painted the features of the Whopper on the side of their buildings? What if you made all your ads the same orange color that the Home Depot uses? You can also use the same type face as well. Then you point out that when it comes to personalized service, this is where the similarity ends.

It just might get you some attention. Who knows? It would be different, wouldn't it?

Just keep mixing all those pieces up and see what you get.

A good example of a product that came out of using Step 2 is the pacifier developed by Cloud International Corp. of Taiwan. I first saw this new product in an issue of *Popular Science*, and right away I wondered why I had never thought of it. After all, I've had four children, and I own a digital thermometer. What Cloud International did was combine a pacifier with a digital thermometer that has a built-in memory. Babies hate having glass thermometers shoved up their butts, but they don't mind having their temperature taken while they're sucking on a pacifier.

Two ideas combined into something new. Not bad, eh?

Here's another neat combination I wish I had dreamed up. Fitness Technologies developed a tiny (2-1/4" x 1-1/2") FM radio for folks who like to whistle while they jog. This is no ordinary radio, though. When you strap it to your waist it will also measure how far you've gone (distance and elapsed time), and how many calories you've burned. In addition, it's a stop watch, *and* it gives you an audible beep to keep you on pace.

All of these things - radio, stopwatch, pedometer, calorie counter, pace setter - have been around for years. These guys paid attention and put them all together.

I have a Timex "Ironman" watch with an Indiglo light that allows me to see the time in the dark. All I have to do is press a tiny button and it lights up. I just spotted a night light in a catalog that works with Indiglo technology. They added a digital clock to the night light so you can tell the time when you wake up to wander around the house, wondering where your next idea will come from.

You know, I've been walking around with that watch on my wrist for at least the past six years. I wish *I* had thought of that night-light idea. I'll just have to pay closer attention!

Anyway, if no new idea strikes you right away, it's probably because you haven't done Step 3 yet.

3. Go do something else for a while. Get all those ideas mixed up in your head, and then forget about them. Go do something else and let your subconscious mind go to work. No one knows why, but it helps if the "something else" you're doing is rhythmic. This might be running, walking, raking the lawn, rocking in a chair, knitting, banging your head against the wall, or whatever. While your body is occupied in a mindless activity, your mind works over the combination. When I have to write a magazine article, I begin the night before by going over my list of technical and people pieces. I'll read through them and just let them float in my subconscious. I'll go to sleep with them on my mind. In the morning, I'll put on my running shoes and go out for a four-mile run though the park. Usually by the second mile, I have the outline of the story in my head. By the fourth mile, it's complete. Then all I have to do is go home, shower, and write it.

I'm constantly amazed at how this method of producing ideas has never let me down.

4. Wait for the idea to come. Which is what I'm doing while I'm sleeping, and then jogging. And don't worry, it *always* comes.

5. Take the idea to others and use their input to develop it into the most useful form possible. The last step applies more to a business decision than it does to article writing. If I'm thinking about a business challenge, I'll take my idea to friends and see what they think (this is one reason why we have trade associations, by the way). My friends give me constructive criticism, which I'll consider and usually take. At the end of the process, I'll have an idea that often works!

Every book I've ever written, every seminar I've ever put together, every business idea I've ever floated began with this process. It's a method that has worked for people since James Webb Young first revealed it in 1940, and you can make it work for you just as well today.

Especially when you combine it with clustering, another very powerful tool.

Clustering - Thinking The Natural Way

The second book I want to tell you about taught me a new way to outline, and it was probably the most eye-opening experience I've ever had.

Remember when you were in grammar school and the teacher taught you how to make an outline? You began with a main subject, which you labeled Roman numeral I. Below this, you listed the items that related to the main subject, giving each a letter of the alphabet. Below the letters, you might have put numbers - 1 2 3 4, and so on.

When you finished with that first subject, you moved on to your second, which you marked with a large Roman numeral II. From there, you continued down the page in a very deliberate way. If you didn't do it this way, the teacher gave you a bad grade so you did what she said.

If you applied that linear way of thinking to your business your outline might look like this.

I. Increase my hydronic heating business

    a. Learn more about hydronics

        1. call local manufacturers reps

        2. send for literature

        3. attend some seminars

    b. Find products that work well together

        1. join trade associations

        2. read more technical articles

        3. talk to my friends in the business

        4. ask a local wholesaler for help

    c. Figure out who my customers are

        1. where do my talents lie?

        2. what do the customers want from me?

            a. what are their problems

d. Find out how to reach customers

    1.   look into advertising that gets me noticed

    2.   put together an interesting sales package that's in the customer's self-interest

That's the way the teacher taught you to do things. Most people don't take the time to do this sort of outline; they just charge out there and start doing business. They make it up as they go along, and they deal with disasters as they occur.

An outline for a business is called a Business Plan, and the trouble with most businesses is that the owner never take the time to make one. But even if you did make one, chances are the Business Plan would follow a linear outline such as the one above.

The trouble with this type of outline is that it's too rigid. It starts at Roman number I and moves on to II and III and IV. But that's not the way people think. Stop for a moment and just think. Go ahead, I'll wait.

THINKING BREAK...

How many thoughts just went through your mind? You probably thought about this book you're reading. You might have wondered what I was up to. Maybe you decided not to stop for a moment and think. You just barged on.

You may have thought about getting a cup of coffee.

You may have thought about what you're going to do later today.

The phone may have called you away.

This is the way people think. You can't hold you mind still for long.

And that's the problem with an outline that moves from I, to II, to III, to IV, and so on. This is not the way your brain works. Your brain flits around like a butterfly in a field of wildflowers. Linear outlines try to put your butterfly in a net.

Which is why the book *Writing the Natural Way* by Gabriele Rico (Houghton Mifflin Company: ISBN 0-87477-236-2) made such an impression on me. It changed the way I think, and the way I work. In the early 1980s, Dr. Rico came up with a new way of drawing an outline. She called it "clustering," because that's what it looks like when you put it on a page. A cluster diagram is nonlinear. It hops all over the page. It's as unorganized as your imagination.

Here's what a cluster diagram of the word **"Contractor"** might look like (as least as it occurs in *my* head).

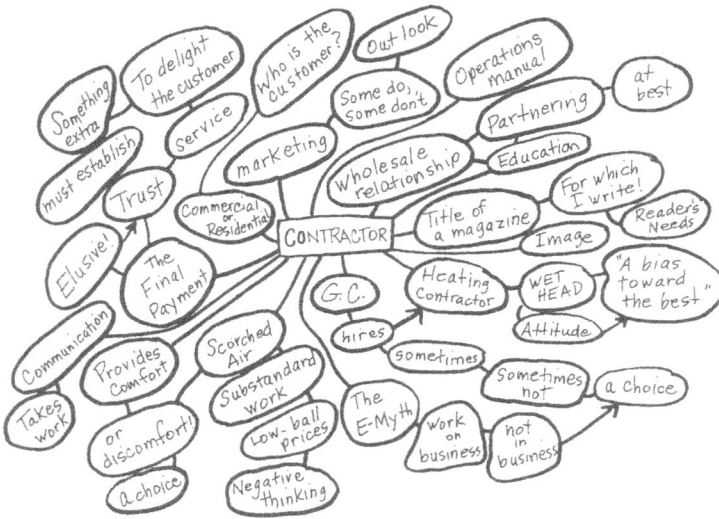

You see, it's the *shape* of the thing that frees up your thoughts. Clustering gives you a way to catch your creative, nonlinear thoughts. I'll admit that when I first saw it, the pattern seemed really disorganized, but then I learned that that's *exactly* what you need to think creatively.

You begin at the center with a core word or phrase, say, **"Increase Hydronic Business."** From there, you very quickly jot down anything that pops into your mind. And I do mean *anything*. Don't put a censor on your brain. Nothing is out of line here. Just let the ideas flow - even if they seem ridiculous. Let you eyes roam over the diagram as it grows and add *whatever* comes to mind. Don't say, Nah, that's stupid. *Just write it down.*

Within a few minutes things will start popping out of your brain that you never even knew were there. This happens because clustering gives you the freedom to hop around. You're not confined to a box. It's like driving a race car in all five gears at the same time. Traditional outlines force you to think in a plodding, straight line. If you get a good idea that doesn't apply to the particular step you've reached, your mind will reject it because it's out of place. You force your brain to say, No! Let's stay focused on the problem! By the time you get to the place where it belongs, you've forgotten it.

Clustering is like having a maniac scampering around the conference table at a formal business meeting. Your little maniac keeps saying things like, "Yeah? Well how about this!" Your maniac won't let you settle on any one thing for too long. That comes later in the process, but right now, he's out of control, and that's a *very* cool thing.

Just write it all down - whatever comes into your mind. And when you're done, you'll find you've uncovered a bunch of great ideas that would not have occurred to you if you were thinking in a straight line. Clustering frees your imagination and your creativity, and because it is so playful, it gives you a way to come up with ideas that are irresistible to regular human beings.

Left Brain, Right Brain

The right side of your brain deals with creative thought; the left side is analytical. If you're trying to figure what's wrong on a job, and you find yourself wandering around, trying to "think" like water, you're using the right side of your brain. Once you figure out what's going on, you sit down and make a list of material you'll have to get. The left side of your brain will take care of that part of the process. The left side is really good at adding up numbers and making lists.

There are, of course, nerves that connect the two sides of your brain together, and signals are constantly shooting back and forth at the speed of light. Thinking requires both sides of your brain, but in a way, they fight each other. The right side says, What if? while the left is saying, Now, slow down there! It reminds me a lot of my marriage. I barge right into things, and I'm always willing to take a chance. That would make me the right side of the brain. The Lovely Marianne, on the other hand, is much more conservative. She actually wants to know what things **cost** before we buy them! Imagine that. If our marriage were a brain, TLM would *definitely* be the left side.

You need both sides to think a thing through, but clustering keeps you on the right side a bit longer than you normally would be. The left side keeps trying to drag you back, make you behave "like an adult." That's why you might feel a thought that belongs in your cluster is stupid. The left side of your brain is telling you that. Ignore Lefty. Just keep jotting down whatever pops into your mind.

Trust Righty.

You'll know you're done with your cluster when you can't write anymore. The feeling you get will be most definite. You'll just know you're done. You'll feel empty.

At that point, use the left side of your brain to make an orderly list of the items in your cluster diagram. This will bring you back to the sort of diagram they taught you to make in grammar school, but it will be much more rich in depth and detail. You'll see.

Now, take a blank piece of paper and make a cluster diagram of the core words, "**Hydronic Comfort.**"

When you're through with that, write the word, "**Advantages**" in the center of another blank piece of paper, and cluster all the advantages a customer will get when she deals with your company.

Now try this. Get more paper and write the word, "**Complaints.**" Cluster every complaint you can think of that a customer has ever made about your company. Organize the list and try to see a pattern. What are you doing that you could be doing better?

Write the word, "**Problem.**" Cluster all the different problems your customers are having.

Take each of those problems and make it a core word. Then cluster the solutions your company can offer. Organize them into a list when you're through.

By the time you're done, you will have a series of outlines around which you can build a very effective advertising campaign for your company.

It didn't cost much to do this, did it?

You should do this at least once a month.

I keep a roll of wrapping paper in my office, which I use to make my cluster diagrams. This book began as a cluster diagram that was two-and-a-half feet high and four feet wide. Every word you're reading sprang from that single diagram.

Every book and every article I've ever written began as a cluster diagram. I take the time to do the diagram because I'm in a hurry. Without the diagram, I wouldn't know where to begin. I'd spend a lot of time staring at a blank computer screen. My diagrams give me a beginning, a middle, and an end. They are my mental road maps, and I would truly be lost without them.

Every seminar I've ever put together started as a cluster diagram. Every business idea I have ever tried began this way as well. It's an amazingly powerful tool, and I hope you put it to good use.

Now, go cluster the word, **"Success!"**

So, How Does It Look?

I received a letter from a contractor who was frustrated because he was having a tough time selling hydronic heat to people who were building high-end homes in his marketing area. "No matter hough hard I try, I jist cant do it. Its because people are to cheep," he wrote.

His letter was on plain white paper, written in pencil. His letterhead was a rubber stamp. I wondered if his proposals for high-end hydronic system looked the same. How must they look to a potential customer? If the contractor can't spell, or doesn't *know* he can't spell, or worse yet, doesn't care that he can't spell, and if he doesn't want to spend a few bucks on business stationary - then what's his work going to look like?

He may be the finest technician in America, his work may be impeccable, but the first impression he gives is that he's sloppy and undereducated. That may not be a fair assessment, but customers have choices, and they make their decisions based largely on the way contractors present themselves. Like it or not.

For me, the saddest part of all of this is that the contractor honestly believes he's losing business because people are cheap.

I've received similar letters on gorgeous letterheads, produced by with laser printers, but nevertheless, shot through with misspelled words and sentences that are nearly incomprehensible. Most word processors have spell-check and grammar-check programs built into them. All you have to do is click on the right icon and the machine will do most of the work for you. And yet, this is still too much trouble for many heating contractors.

Like it or not, the way you present yourself in writing is every bit as important as the way you present yourself in person. Misspelled words are as noticeable as a butt crack.

One contractor told me he's a contractor not a writer. "I've never been able to spell," he said, almost proudly. "People judge me by my *work*, not by my writing." And then he told me he didn't get much of the higher-end hydronic work because it cost too much - and because people are cheap.

This is your competition.

Think you can take him?

If you don't want to take the time to learn how to write business letters and proposals, hire someone to do it for you and add the costs of their services to your overhead when you're figuring your prices.

You only get one chance to make a first impression.

8

The Hinge Principle

A story for your consideration:

It took Mel a half-hour to realize the home owner hadn't understood a word he had said. "It was like explaining clouds to fish," he told his partner Larry. "But I got all the way up to the part about the reset control before I realized that," he said. "And even at that point, the guy was *still* nodding. A real *fast* nod, too. I thought I was doing okay because of the smile and the nod, you know?" Mel bobbed his head like one of those plastic dogs people put by the rear windows of their cars. Larry bobbed in response. Watching Mel, he couldn't help but bob.

"He didn't understand *anything* you told him?" Larry asked incredulously, his head continuing to waggle.

"Seems so!" Mel said, "But I didn't find out until the end. I *hate* that." Mel rubbed the back of his neck. "It was a *total* waste of time."

"What made you think he understood you in the first place?" Larry asked, upset that Mel had once again failed to ring the bell on what would have been a really nice job.

"Well, he told me I was the fifth heating contractor he was interviewing. I *hate* when they put it that way - *interviewing*. It makes it sound like I'm there looking for a job."

"You *were* there looking for a job," Larry reminded him.

"Yeah, but it's not like I was looking for a *job* job. I just wanted to sell him a hydronic heating system. I wasn't planning to make a career out of the thing. And besides, I figured since I was the fifth guy in there, he probably knew what he was looking for. I mean, the guy's building a heck of a big house. I figured he should know what he wants."

"I would have felt the same way," Larry said. "So tell me, how did you explain what we were going to do for him?"

"Well, first I showed him the specifications on the boiler we were going to use, and I explained that this boiler gives great AFUE."

"And what did he say to that?"

"He smiled and he nodded," Mel said. "Just like I told you."

"Did you tell him what AFUE stood for?"

"I figured he knew!" Mel said, shaking his head in frustration. "I was the fifth guy in there, for Pete's sake! And besides, he kept nodding and smiling, you know?"

"Uh huh," Larry said, "I would have figured the same thing. What happened then?"

"Well, I showed him a picture of the radiant tubing we were planning on using, and I told him how our system was going to balance out the MRT in his new home."

"What did he say?"

"He just nodded. It was like he had a hinge in the back of his neck. His head just kept going up and down, and he kept smiling like a happy idiot."

"And then?"

"I showed him the DIN standard for the tubing, and I told him how the manufacturer we use meets that standard, and that everything was going to be just fine."

"Did he know what the DIN standard was?"

"He seemed to," Mel said. "I mean, I didn't *tell* him or anything. I figured he *must* have known because of the way he was nodding and all. And besides, he had talked to all those other guys before me, right?"

Larry nodded. "You're right. So what happened next?"

"I looked at the plans and explained about the available emissive surfaces in the rooms. I explained how we might have to supplement with a water-to-air heat exchanger on a separate zone because of the R-value of all the glass he was planning to use, and how we had to get the CFM just right. He kept nodding and smiling. The more I talked, the faster he nodded."

"Did you explain about how we install bimetal thermometers to monitor the delta-T?"

"I sure did! And I told him about the variable delta-P as well, and how we were going to handle that with a DPR.

He nodded at that too. I asked if any of the other four contractors were going to do it that way."

"What did he say?"

"He just nodded and smiled."

"Did you tell him how we were going to control the heat in the kids' bedrooms?" Larry asked.

"With the TRVs? Yeah, I told him all about the TRVs, and how the ones we use respond with just a four-degree P-deviation. Can't do better than a four-degree P-deviation."

"And?"

"And he nodded. I thought he was impressed by the four-degree P-deviation. Hey, it impressed the hell out of me!"

"So when did you tell him about the reset control?"

"Right after I explained about the microbubbles. How you can't see them, but that we were going to get rid of them anyway."

"That's great," Larry said. "But what about the reset? What went wrong?"

"Well, as soon as I mentioned the reset control I realized the guy hadn't understood a word I had said to him. I'd been talking to a total dummy! When I started to tell him how the water temperature would get colder as it got warmer outside, he nodded faster than ever, but he also put his hands up. He told me he doesn't like to take cold showers, no matter how warm it is outside. Can you believe it?"

"It is hard to believe," Larry said. "Did you try to explain?"

"I tried to tell him about Proportional plus Integral plus Derivative and all, but he wouldn't listen to me anymore. He thanked me for coming, and walked me to the door, nodding all the way. I mean, the guy was just so unbelievably stupid, you know?" Mel shook his head. "I don't think he understood a word I had said, but you'd never know that by the way he was nodding. It was like he had a hinge in his neck. A regular hinge!"

"You think maybe you were too technical with him? Maybe he didn't understand, but he just didn't want you to know that, so he nodded instead?"

Mel considered this for a moment and then said, "Hey, I was the *fifth* guy in there. That bozo shoulda done his homework. The way I figure it, if you're gonna buy a hydronic heating system, you oughta learn to speak the language. I got no sympathy for that loser, none whatsoever."

Larry paused a moment, considering this, and then he nodded in agreement

FM Transmitters and AM Receivers

I wrote that story about Larry and Mel (a couple of guys who were born in a cluster diagram) after seeing it happen to so many contractors in real life. These guys fell in love with the technology, learned all about it, and then assumed everyone in the world knew about it too. They tried to sell the features instead of the benefits.

A contractor friend from Queens, New York, gave me the title for that story. "When the home owner starts nodding his head you should *always* stop talking."

"Why?" I asked.

"Because of the Hinge Principle," he said.

"What's that?"

"It's a human nature thing," he explained. "When someone doesn't know what you're talking about, and you happen to be trying to sell that person something, he will nod."

"Nod?" I said.

"Yes, nod. They will nod because they don't want you to get the upper hand. If you know more about the subject in a technical way, the person you are trying to sell will think you are going to screw him. So he will nod to make you think he is as tuned in as your are. It is the rare home owner who will not nod when you start to talk too technical."

"You've found this to be true in Queens?" I asked.

He smiled. "I've found this to be true *everywhere*, Dan. And the faster they nod, the *less* they understand. This is the Hinge Principle! And if you don't stop talking about whatever it is that's making the guy nod, you're going to be standing out on the street wondering what happened to you."

There. Sage advice, free for the taking.

Someone else described this process as having an FM transmitter when all the home owners have AM receivers

"You could be playing the most beautiful music," he said, "but they're not tuned to your station."

Wet Heads listen to FM, but *always* transmit on AM.

How To Improve Your Reception

I was doing a seminar on hydronic radiant heat for a group of contractors during the summer of 1996. We were in a resort hotel on the beach at Ocean City, Maryland, a glorious place you should visit at least once in your lifetime.

This place has an indoor ice skating rink in the lobby, just a few hundred feet from the ocean. You can sun yourself all morning, and skate all afternoon, if the spirit moves you. Our meeting room was right next to the ice skating rink, and as the attendees arrived in their tee shirts and shorts (it was a *very* casual seminar), they complained about how cold it was when they walked by the rink.

Now, that morning I was faced with the task of having to explain to these people that hydronic radiant heat is different from any other type of heating system. Hydronic radiant heat controls the heat loss from your *body*, not the heat loss from the room. With hydronic radiant heat, you're trying to get the temperature of the surfaces of the room as close as possible to the temperature of the *outside* of the clothed human body, that being about 85-degrees Fahrenheit. You do this because the human body is a radiator that generates heat. Half the heat you lose leaves your body as radiant energy, moving toward things that are cooler than 85-degrees F. When you control the rate of heat loss from the body, you control that person's level of comfort.

This is the key to understanding hydronic radiant heat. It's why engineers use a different type of heat loss calculation when they size a hydronic radiant heating system. They're not concerned with heating air. In fact, in a room that's heated with a hydronic radiant system, the air temperature at the ceiling will be almost identical to the air temperature just above the floor.

And since the air temperature at the ceiling is relatively cool, the heat loss from the room is less. There's also less heat loss from infiltration in a room heated with hydronic radiant heat, and that's what makes these systems so efficient. A well-designed hydronic radiant system can save as much as 40 percent on the fuel usage, compared to a scorched-air system.

But the key to understanding this - and to marketing it - is to think of the human body as a radiator, and forget about heating the air. This is a tough one for heating contractors to grasp, let alone home owners.

At my seminar, I decided to use the ice skating rink to make this point. I waited until the last attendee had arrived. He grabbed a cup of coffee and complained about how chilly it was out at the rink.

When everyone was seated I asked them what temperature they thought it was in the conference room. Their guesses ranged from 68 to 72 degrees F. I took out a digital thermometer and checked. The temperature was exactly 70 degrees. "Not bad!" I said. "You were all very close."

"That's because we're in the business," one guy offered. "We get calls from people all the time who complain that it's too cold. But when we get there we can feel that's it's 70 degrees. And when we check, it's usually within a degree. You get so you can be as accurate as a thermometer when you're in the business long enough."

"I'm glad to hear that," I said. "What temperature do you suppose it is out by the ice skating rink?" They all started to laugh. "It can't be more than 60 degrees out there," a woman offered with a shiver. "I'd agree with her," a man said. The others nodded.

"Let's check it out," I said, picking up the digital thermometer.

We all traipsed out to the rink and I held the thermometer's probe about a foot off the surface of the ice. The skaters stared at us as though we were nuts.

"It's 76-degrees," I announced.

"No way!" one guy shouted. "Let me see that." I handed him the thermometer and let him check for himself. The others gathered around, and each had a turn to take a good look.

"Want to go back inside?" I asked.

"Yeah," the woman said, "it's too cold here!"

"It's 76 degrees here," I said.

"I don't care what that thermometer says," she laughed. "I'm cold!" She scurried back to get another cup of coffee in our relatively "warm" conference room where the temperature was only 70 degrees.

Now that I had their attention, I told them about a phenomenon called "Cold-70." It's the feeling you get when there's a big difference between the air temperature and the temperature of the surfaces around you. This is because your body is a "radiator," and it will radiate its heat toward anything that's colder than it is. When you stand next to cold objects, your body's heat loss increases and you feel uncomfortable, even though the air might be 72 degrees F.

Engineers have talked about this for more than 60 years. It's what often makes a scorched air system feel so uncomfortable, while a hydronic radiant floor feel so good.

"That's the way you market hydronic radiant heat to your customers," I told them.

"We have to take them to a skating rink?" one of the guys asked. "We don't have one of those in our town."

"No, not a skating rink," I said. "A food store."

"A food store?"

"Yes, a food store. Grab your thermometer and walk them up and down the aisles. Most food stores have scorched air heating systems. When you get to the frozen food aisle, you and your customer will feel the same way you just did when you stood next to the ice rink. Take the temperature of the air in the frozen food aisle and show them it's the same as it is in every other aisle. That's the best way to sell hydronic radiant heat."

"But what if they don't want to go with me to the food store?" a guy in the back asked.

"Then you paint a word picture - just as I have here."

People who are good at marketing hydronic heat do that. They paint beautiful word pictures that connect things people know intuitively with the technical aspects of hydronic heat. They focus on the *benefits*, the way the system makes you *feel*. They market what hydronics *does*, not what it *is*.

You can do that, can't you?

Sure you can!

How You Might Market Multiple-Boiler Systems

One boiler is better than two. Two are better than three. You know why? Because if one should break down, you always have another. Just about everybody can grasp that logic. That's why the insurance industry does so well. We live under the weight of the What if? question.

Hospitals have more than one boiler, so do schools, nursing homes, military bases. I've been in the homes of many rich people. Most have more than one boiler. Even the rich folks that lived at the turn of the century had more than one boiler. It's not a new concept. It's like wearing a belt and suspenders.

But the other reason for having more than one boiler makes even more sense than the insurance reason - it doesn't get that cold every day. When you have a multiple-boiler system, you put just the amount of heat you need into the building. If you pipe the system with primary/secondary pumping techniques, you'll *really* have something to brag about because no water will flow though a boiler when it's off. That saves money.

You know all this because you're in the business, and manufacturers have been shoving multiple boiler systems at you for a number of years. You realize that when you size one of these systems, you're not oversizing the job. When you add the capacity of all the boilers, the total equals, but doesn't exceed, the needs of the building on the coldest day of the year. So, for instance, if the building needs, say 300,000 BTUH, you might install two, 150,000 BTUH boilers, or three 100,000 BTUH boilers. You'll spend more on boilers, sure, but for most of the year, you'll be firing just one of those little boilers instead of a single big one.

Now how do you market this to a customer who doesn't speak the language of hydronics?

I've had good luck asking them how much clothing they have in their closets. Usually, they laugh and say something like, "A lot!"

Then I ask them why they have a lot of clothing and they look at me like I've lost my mind, but they usually play along. "So I don't have to wear the same thing every day," they say.

"What do you wear on a mild day?" I ask.

"A light jacket. Maybe a sweater."

"And on a frigid day?"

"Oh, I dress in layers, and put on a heavy coat, some gloves, a hat, you know."

"Ever think about dressing that way every day of the winter?" I ask.

"No! That would be crazy!"

"Why?"

"Because it doesn't get that cold every day of the winter. Why would I want to wear all my clothes on a mild day?"

From this point, it's pretty easy to make the jump to a multiple-boiler system. Why wear all your boilers when it's not that cold outside?

You can do this, can't you? Sure you can!

How You Might Market Outdoor-Reset

You have cruise-control on your car? That's outdoor reset. No matter how often conditions change, reset keeps your hydronic system cruising along with just enough power to meet the needs of the moment. And like cruise-control, it saves energy.

How am I doing?

How You Might Market An Indirect Water Heater

When The Lovely Marianne and I bought our house in 1978 it came with a circa 1950 American Standard Arcoliner boiler with a tankless coil. This boiler had two clean-out doors, each larger than the door on our oven. You could store all your summer clothes inside that boiler and still have room for snow shovels. The fittings that connected the tankless coil to the half-inch copper tubing had what looked like white and green mushrooms growing on them. Very scary.

We could take a shower courtesy of that old tankless coil, but while doing so we'd better not turn on the thermostat, or run water in the sink, or start the washing machine.

We rationed our hot water like hillbillies.

"It's your turn to take a shower," I'd say.

"Okay, don't make any coffee until I get out," she'd answer.

"Okay."

And then our four daughters tumbled out of heaven and suddenly we were running that shower a lot more. Our daughters spend more time in the water than Flipper. We needed to do something, and we needed to do it fast!

We wound up getting a new, fuel-efficient boiler, and an indirect water heater. We installed the indirect water heater in a closet on the second floor of the house because we don't have a basement, and the boiler room is tight for space. That's one of the nice things about an indirect water heater; you can put it just about anywhere. Make sure you tell your customer that.

But the best part was our new indirect heater held enough water to let all these young women shower while the clothes washer was going, and the dish washer as well. We were even able to heat the house at the same time!

Now, you know what a Thermos is, don't you? Well, an indirect water heater is very similar to that. Picture a big, heavily insulated tank filled with water. This tank has a copper coil inside of it, and we run boiler water through that coil to heat the domestic water. The two waters never touch each other, and everything stays very clean. (How am I doing?)

There's no burner inside the indirect water heater so it will last much longer than a standard water heater. There's also no chimney running up through it, so the water stays hotter - just like it does in a Thermos.

You get it? Home owners may not know what an indirect water heater is, but they've all seen a Thermos. I'm taking something they *don't* know and attaching it to something they *do* know.

But before I do that, I'm identifying a problem most people have (not enough hot water). I'm telling a story about my life as a regular human being, and once they begin to identify with me, I tell them how I solved the problem. I connect the new thing to the known thing, and suddenly they feel very comfortable with indirect heaters, as well as anything thing else hydronic.

Who knows? They may even want you to install an indirect water heater. They may also ask for a warm floor courtesy of a couple of boilers operating on outdoor reset. That's what happens when you learn how to market hydronic comfort. All you have to do is sell what hydronics *does*, not what it *is*. Keep your language simple by using stories. Paint beautiful word pictures. Attach things they don't know to things they do know. And, most of all, be wildly enthusiastic.

You can do that, can't you? Sure you can!

Our men will be at your home at 8 a.m, and not sooner because we want to give your family a chance to get off to work and school before we start your job.

The Incredible Power
of Word Pictures

Few people like to do major construction on their homes. A hydronic heating system is a somewhat major project, so when it's time to change a boiler or install a new hydronic radiant system for that addition, home owners usually have some concerns about how you're going to do things.

You feel the same way, don't you? I mean if you were going into the hospital for surgery you would want the doctor to take the time to explain the procedure to you beforehand, wouldn't you?

A Wet Head does this by painting word pictures.

Imagine if you gave your customer a letter that read something like this.

"Our men will be at your home at 8 AM, and not sooner because we want to give your family a chance to get off to work and school before we start your job. Our men won't park in your driveway without your permission, and they'll be sure to lay drop cloths on your walkway and floors to

protect your belongings. We'll treat your home with the same care we'd give our own.

None of our people will smoke or use foul language in your home. That's not our style; we'll treat you with the respect you deserve.

We'll be very careful when we remove your old heating equipment, and when we're through, we promise to leave the work area cleaner than we found it."

And so on . . . Get the picture?

What sort of an impression do you think you'll make on your new customer when you show her this letter during your sales call? Do you think it might give you an edge? Do you think it might give her second thoughts about your lower-priced competitor?

And what effect do you think a letter such as this will have on your own people? It's a nice way of letting them know what you expect from them, isn't it? It's a subtle way of raising the bar.

Take The Time To Tell Your Story

When you do a good job of telling your story - when you create good images in people's minds by painting powerful word pictures - people naturally want to do business with you. There is proof of this everywhere you look.

Not long ago I was flying on a USAir jet. I was a bit anxious because USAir had just had a jet go down, but they were the only realistic option I had to get from where I was to where I needed to be.

I buckled myself in and opened the in-flight magazine to the editorial page. I'm always interested in what the head of an airline has to say. Seth Schofield, who is the Chairman and CEO of USAir, wanted to reassure me that the airplane I was on was safe. Here, in part, is what he has to say under the headline,

Overnight At The Airport

"Tonight for example, this airplane or one like it will drop off its last passengers sometime after midnight. As quiet settles over the concourse and the last passenger strides away, the empty airplane is slowly pushed back from the gate.

"The ramp tug moves the plane down the ramp, across the apron, onto the taxiway, and out to the line maintenance hanger, often across the field.

"There, the hanger's massive four-story doors rumble aside. High-intensity light spills into the night while the tug backs the plane into its space beside four or five other aircraft recently deposited for service.

"Inside, a highly skilled team of mechanics and technicians is ready to check, remove, replace, install or just plain fix what might be ailing - and do the inspections and other work dictated by rigorous federal and company regulations.

"They tackle the aircraft routine maintenance checks and preventative tasks, as well as the work generated by the day's flying and reported by the pilots and flight attendants who operate the plane. The comprehensive work performed throughout the night helps minimize any unforeseen mechanical delay that could hold back on-time takeoffs the following day."

He didn't say anything about plane crashes, just that they do this to avoid on-time delays. But it sure made me feel better, and I'm sure that was his goal.

Notice the imagery he created by describing the "massive four-story doors rumbling aside" and the "high-intensity light spilling into the night." He doesn't have a bunch of wrench jockeys, he has a "highly skilled team of mechanics and technicians."

Everyone's watching over this plane I'm sitting in - the federal government, the company, the pilot, the flight attendants, the highly skilled team of mechanics and technicians, me.

How could this plane possibly crash?

This is the power of a well-told story.

You can create the same sort of magic around *your* company if you really want to.

Consider this, for instance. You thirsty?

Drink Birch Beer!

I was sitting in a restaurant outside of Albuquerque, New Mexico, trying to decide what drink to order with my lunch (it was too early for beer).

I spotted a tent card on the table that read,

Brewsters Old-Fashioned, Genuine Draft, Keg Birch Beer
You've never tasted anything like it!
Non-alcoholic, caffeine-free, hand-crafted, micro-brewed.

I turned the card over and read this story while I was waiting for the waitress.

"K.C. Brewster's special memories as a kid are of the warm summer nights when he'd get to help Grandaddy brew birch beer.

"They'd sneak out back behind the smokehouse in their sleepy Pennsylvania town, to keep the Brewster family's recipe secret. Once word got out they were fix'n a batch, the whole town would show up for a taste.

"The excitement of rolling the seasoned birchwood kegs to the fire was only heightened by the rich smell of the wood in the country night air.

"Today, K.C. Brewster uses the same childhood wonder and natural ingredients as he microbrews the famous family recipe. Today there is plenty of his foamy birch beer for the whole neighborhood to enjoy. Now you can have the rich taste of K.C. Brewster's Old Fashioned Keg Birch Beer without all that sneaking around back."

I ordered one, of course. It was damn fine birch beer, and I wouldn't have known about it had it not been for that little tent card.

Which got me thinking.

Suppose you made an arrangement with a local diner in your town. Say, you take care of some or all of their service needs they may have in exchange for them placing a tent card on their tables.

Maybe your tent card has a message such as this.

Ah, the warmth of the sun. All winter long!

You flip it over and read,

"When I was a boy Mom and Dad would take us to Grandma and Grandpa's house for the holidays. While the grown-ups were preparing the table for dinner, my brother and I would curl up on the throw rug in front of the old cast-iron radiator and listen to the carolers on the radio.

"That radiator shined such a wonderful warmth on us! I never felt anything quite like it again until I installed hydronic radiant floor heating in our home.

"A warm floor greets you like an old friend when you come in from the cold. It warms without overheating. There are no drafts, no hot and cold spots, no radiators to keep clean, and hydronic radiant comfort has lowered our family's fuel bill by an impressive amount.

"But best of all, our family now enjoys this almost indescribable feeling of comfort that says, Welcome home. All winter long!

"I can install this sort of comfort in your home too."

And then you put your name and telephone number on the bottom of the card.

What do you think? You're catching people as they sit down to enjoy a meal. They've just come in out of the cold. They're probably putting up with the restaurant's noisy, dusty, scorched air system while they're reading your card. They've probably been next to an old cast-iron radiator at some point in their lives.

Don't you think this would be worth a try?

This is what Wet Heads do. This is what makes them *different*.

Eat Steak!

Have you ever had the pleasure of dining at a Ruth's Chris Steak House? This is a place where you will pay about twenty-five bucks for a piece of meat. It comes on a plate with a sprig of parsley. If you want a potato, well, that's extra. So is everything else.

And you'd better have a reservation because people are waiting in long lines to pay those prices for a meal.

These, by the way, are the same folks *some* contractors insist won't spend extra money on their heating systems. Wet Heads know that's not true.

Anyway, here's how Ruth's Chris Steak House gets you.

"Premium steak never goes out of style. Enjoy aged Ruth's Chris steak, broiled at 1800 degrees to lock in the corn-fed flavor . . . served sizzling. Come help us celebrate 30 sizzling years. And come hungry!"

Every restaurant *cooks* their steaks. Ruth's Chris dares to be different *by broiling at 1800 degrees* to lock in the corn-fed flavor.

What temperature does the other guy use?

No one knows, right? It might even be 1800 degrees, but at this point, if they say it's 1800 degrees, they're going to look like a Me Too! business.

Ruth's Chris built a business by being specific about the temperature of their broiler.

Suppose you were to tell a customer that you soldered all your fittings at a certain temperature to make sure the joints held fast. Or that you used only lead-free solder. Or that the burners you used produced only a certain decibel level.

There's a power in giving details - especially if you get passionate about your subject.

Look at what Lands End has managed to do with detailed descriptions of their boat shoes and other products. How can they charge more? They make their products more interesting.

No, Eat Fish!

Here's another example of the same thing. Legal Sea Foods is a chain of fabulously successful restaurants in New England, and again, you'd best have reservations if you want to get in any time soon.

While I was waiting for our waitress, I read my place mat and learned these interesting things about Legal Sea Foods.

- *Legal Sea Food's own buyers hand select all our seafood, fresh off the boat. Almost 75 tons a week!*

- *During the year, we select from over 40 varieties of fish, more than any other restaurant in the country.*

- *We require all our employees who handle food, from the person who cuts the fish to the person who makes the salads, to wear surgical rubber gloves.*

- *We are the only seafood restaurant in the country with an in-house laboratory for testing shellfish on a daily basis. We are participating in a pilot seafood inspection program (HACCP) sponsored by the FDA, which the U.S. Government hopes to implement across the United States.*

- *We use our own water-filtration system in every store and restaurant. The purified water is used for ice, soda and coffee.*

I felt pretty good about the quality of the fish I was about to order. It was from this place mat that I got the idea of how a Wet Head might explain how the job was going to go to a customer. Remember?

"Our men will be at your home at 8 AM, and not sooner because we want to give your family a chance to get off to work and school before we start your job. Our men won't park in your driveway without your permission, and they'll be sure to lay drop cloths on your walkway and floors to protect your belongings. We'll treat our home with the same care we'd give our own."

And so on. You don't have to be an original; you just have to pay attention to what works, and then adapt it to your business by giving it your own special twist.

You can do that, can't you? Sure you can!

Dear Guest

While you're paying attention to other businesses, notice how the policies of some do a fantastic job of making you angry from the first moment you meet. They think they have good reason to do this. They've been treated unfairly by some of their customers in the past, so they treat all their *new* customers as if they were adversaries.

For instance, I stayed at the Bel Aire Hotel in Erie, PA not long ago. Nice people at the desk, and a good clean room, but once I set down my suitcase, this is what I found.

On the dresser there was a sign that read,

Dear Guest,

For your convenience we have irons and ironing boards available at the front desk. Please do not use the room furniture as an alternative. Dial extension 720 or 0 for this service.

I felt like my mother was talking to me. But that wasn't all. Over on the desk there was a small tent card. It read, *ATTENTION! Please do not tamper with FIRE DETECTORS. Please alert front desk if a problem arises.*

I had no intention of tampering with the fire detectors. Besides I figure it's the guys who are ironing the furniture that are most likely tampering with the fire detectors. That didn't stop the staff of the Bel Aire hotel from yelling at me, though.

My favorite sign was in the bathroom. This one read,

Dear Guest,

Due to the popularity of our guest room terry cloth items, our front desk in the main lobby now offers these items for sale:

Bath Towels $10.00

Hand Towels $ 6.00

Wash Cloths $3.00

Each guest room attendant is responsible for maintaining the guest room items. If you take a towel to the pool or sauna please be sure and return the towel to your room. Should you decide to take these articles from your room, instead of obtaining them at the front desk, we will assume you approve a corresponding charge to your account.

In other words, they know I'm a thief, and this is their way of warning me. Made me feel real welcome.

Finally, they left me a coupon for a free breakfast. Here's how they offered it.

Please join us for a FREE continental breakfast in Maxi's Cafe from the hours of 6 - 10 AM. Present this coupon to your server. Gratuities Not Included. This coupon may be used as a $1.25 credit toward the purchase of any breakfast item. Not redeemable for cash or cash equivalent.

They give me something for nothing, tell me it's worth a buck and a quarter, and that I'd better leave a tip.

Gosh, what a deal!

Now, suppose they had handled things this way instead.

Dear Guest,

For your convenience we have irons and ironing boards available at the front desk. There's no charge, of course, for this additional service. We want you to look your best. Just call and we'll rush one right up to you!

Or how about this version of the fire detector sign.

FOR YOUR SAFETY, we have installed a fire and smoke detection system throughout the Bel Aire hotel. This system is self-contained and fully automatic. It will sound in the event of smoke or fire. Please let the front desk know if you're having a problem with the system. Thanks!

As for the towels, doesn't this sound better?

*OUR GUESTS **LOVE** OUR TOWELS! So much so that they often like to show their friends back home what true terry cloth luxury is all about. Help yourself to as many of our towels as you'd like. We've priced them right, and you can conveniently charge them to your account. Just let us know at check-out what items you've selected.*

Bath Towels $10.00

Hand Towels $ 6.00

Wash Cloths $3.00

Sounds better than calling you a stinking thief, doesn't it? I sure think so.

I've stayed at the Sheraton Portsmouth Hotel & Conference in New Hampshire many times. I get a kick out of what they say on this plastic card I always find in their bathrooms.

Dear Guest,

For your convenience, this room has been equipped with a hair dryer and iron. The hair dryer has been placed on the bathroom vanity. The iron and full-size ironing board are located in the guest room closet.

We check these items daily, however, please advise us at extension 887 if an item is missing upon your arrival.

Thank you,

Housekeeping Services.

How's that? They know *I'm* not a thief, but they're not so sure about the last guy who stayed here. Made me feel a *lot* better. I wouldn't trust that bum either.

See? It's not just *what* you say, it's *how* you say it. Take a close look at every proposal and contract you show to your potential customers. Try to see it through their eyes. You might be saying something between the lines that's turning them off.

Take a look at your boiler-plate Contract. Why not call it an Agreement instead? Doesn't that sound better? Isn't it less threatening?

And how about the words "Total Payment" down there at the bottom of that contract. Having to make a TOTAL PAYMENT sort of makes you feel as though you just made a total mistake, doesn't it? Suppose you changed "Total Payment" to "Your Investment." Doesn't that sound better down there on that bottom line?

Give it some thought.

Take a close look at the way you word everything you do. Those words on the paper may be scaring customers away at the last minute. Words are powerful things.

Be An Imagineer

(I ended my book Pumping Away with these words. After rereading them, I realized these words belong in this book as well.)

If you were water, which way would you go? If you were air, could you get out? What does a BTU look like? How big is it? If you could hold it in your hand, what would it feel like? How much would it weigh? What color is it?

These are some of the questions imagineers ask themselves. Imagineers like to pretend they're inside the pipes, riding the water in a rubber boat. When they're troubleshooting, they take a mental walk through the system and think like water and air. Which way would *I* go if I were the water? If I were air, could I get out of here?

Imagineers think in simple terms. They look at **systems**, not just symptoms, and they take things one step at a time. They're very effective troubleshooters because they take the time to think, *really think*, about what's going on. And they fully define the problem before trying to solve it. And they have fun.

They consider the color and the weight and the texture of British Thermal Units and other things that don't exist because they know there will be days when they'll have to explain invisible things such as these to people who know *nothing* about heating, but who might buy something from them - if only the imagineer can make them *see* what's going on.

An imagineer might light a match and let it burn unil it reaches the very tip of his finger. The customer will watch, sitting on the edge of his seat. "That's a single BTU," the imagineer will say. "When your burner comes on, it will be like 7,500 **books** of matches, all flaring up at the same instant. Imagine that power!"

Imagineers paint word pictures. People love word pictures.

A clever imagineer might say, "The BTUs ride the water like a passenger on a train. They get on in the boiler and off in the radiators. I size the pipe properly so all the passengers can fit on the train." The home owner nods his head in understanding.

When discussing a radiant floor heating system, an imagineer talks about supermarkets and freezers and the human body as a radiator - things people can wrap their minds around. A good imagineer never forgets that people don't buy boilers and pumps and valves and controls. They buy comfort. They buy what this stuff *does*, not what it *is*. Can you see that?

People buy things that are as intangible as a BTU.

So think a little bit every day. Do it in the bathroom. The bathroom is inspirational! Let the hot water beat down on your head, and don't talk to anyone, or listen to the radio. Just think!

Do it every day. It adds up, with interest.

And get enthusiastic. Enthusiasm is positively contagious. Always remember, there are no boring subjects. There are only boring people.

I once met a man who was passionate about ice because that's what he sold. Ice fed his family. He talked to me about clarity and the lack of bubbles in his ice. He explained how his packaging kept his ice from dripping all over my car. He talked about the size and shape of cubes and how his fit through the narrow neck of sports bottles. The guy was passionate about ice. He waved his arms around and smiled a crazy grin.

The ice man made me see the magic in ice.

There are no boring subjects, there are only boring people who hate their jobs. And boring people are as contagious as enthusiastic people. You can catch one or the other just as easily. It's all up to you.

So think a little bit every day about the way you spend your working hours, and why you do things the way you do them. Think about the Dead Men who came before you, and give yourself a half-hour every week to think about the business you're *really* in.

Use your imagination, it's a precious gift from God. Remember how fertile that imagination was when you were a little kid. Strive to bring it back to that same level. It takes practice, but boy it's fun!

Do this now: Think about what a British Thermal Unit looks like, how big it is, what is feels like, how much it weighs, what color it is. And when you've got it all figured out, go describe it to some little kid. Don't stop describing until you make her see that BTU in her mind's eye. Make that kid smile with delight.

Then go talk to the people. They'll hear the pictures in your head, and they'll buy what you're selling: ***Comfort!***

There are no boring subjects. There are only boring people.

10

So They've Called You...

Cool! But what do you do now?

Since you're reading this book I shouldn't have to tell you about bad breath and butt cracks. I also shouldn't have to tell you about parking your truck in their driveway (without their permission) or being on time for your appointment. You've already gotten rid of your political bumper stickers, the *Penthouse* air fresheners hanging from your rear view mirror, and your truck is clean.

The next thing you have to do is listen carefully, and don't screw up.

What Fred Said

My friend Fred heads up the Corporate Communications Department at a big New York City corporation. He's in charge of a TV studio and he knows more about modern communications technology than anyone I've ever met. He loves to share what he knows, and I always learn something when I'm with him by shutting up and listening.

I also ask for his advice from time to time.

I needed a new TV for the den a few years ago, and since Fred had stopped by for a visit, I asked for his recommendation.

"What size do you want?" he asked.

"Just like a twenty-inch," I said, not wanting to go crazy.

"You want something with a really nice picture and sound in that size?"

"Sure."

"How much you wanna spend?"

"Maybe three, four-hundred," I said.

"Okay, get a pen and write this down." I did, and he gave me the model number of a Mitsubishi. "This one just got great reviews in the trade magazines. You won't be sorry. I'll look forward to watching it when I come over."

That weekend, The Lovely Marianne and I went to our local appliance super store to buy the Mitsubishi. Since I already knew exactly what I wanted, I figured I'd shop just for price. I walked in and a salesman flew across the floor and attached himself to us. "How can I help you?" he asked with a smile that reached right around and grabbed at my wallet.

"I'm interested in a price on this Mitsubishi," I said, handing him the piece of paper with the model number.

He looked at it and said, "Sony has a much better model. It's right over here. Let me show it to you."

"But I'm really interested in the Mitsubishi. You do sell Mitsubishi, don't you? I saw a sign in the window."

"Oh, we sell Mitsubishi, but their TVs are no way as good as Sony's. Let me show you why."

"But I was told to get the Mitsubishi," I said.

"Let me show you the Sony. You'll see the difference right away." He walked toward the Sony section and gestured for us to follow, which we did. He launched into a technical lecture neither of us understood. When he was through, I asked him to show us the Mitsubishi.

"The Sony's better," he said.

We walked out of the store.

That afternoon we went to a smaller store that has been in the neighborhood for as long as I can remember. "Do you have this Mitsubishi TV?" I asked, handing the guy the piece of paper. "Yes," he said.

"May we see it?"

"Of course."

When he was through showing us the TV we really wanted he began to explain how his company stands behind every product they sell. If we ever had a problem we could call their service department and they would send someone to fix it. He told us they would be happy to deliver the TV the next day if we didn't want to take it with us. He handed us his business card after writing his home telephone number on it. "If you ever have a problem with anything you buy here, you may call me at home if the store's not open."

He asked how long we planned to keep the TV (as long as possible), and then showed us an extended-service warrantee. He showed us a binder in which he kept letters from satisfied buyers of the plan (all local people). He got truly excited as he explained the story behind a few of the letters. "This guy is from my church," he said, pointing at the hand-written note. "He was really happy he had the plan because the set broke a month after the factory warranty ran out. That doesn't happen too often with Mitsubishi, but you never know."

He asked if we needed any other appliances, and told us he could give us a great deal on a package.

Lesson? When your customer already knows what he wants, give it to him - and then add to the order by suggesting things that are in his self-interest.

Had I bought any TV other than that *specific* Mitsubishi, Fred would have wondered why I asked for his advice - and then didn't take it. If I ever had a problem with that Sony, Fred would have smirked for at least five years.

Who needs that?

If the customer asks specifically for a, say, Weil-McLain it may be because his brother works at the factory in Michigan City. Or maybe the guy has stock in the company. Maybe he grew up with a Weil-McLain in his ancestral home and he wants to keep the family tree pure. Who the heck knows?

Don't tell him he's nuts for wanting what he wants.

You might as well call him a jerk.

Why I'm Now Driving A Minivan

I was in the market for a new van. For four years I'd been driving a beautiful red- and-bronze Ford Club Wagon Chateau that had more options than Lou Holtz. I'd bought it off the lot at the end of the model year in 1992, and I'd gotten a really good deal. But now that it had 84,000 hard miles on it, I figured it was time for a new one.

The Lovely Marianne and I docked our aging, but still regal, Club Wagon Chateau in front of the dealer's showroom window and strolled in. A nice young man named John bounded out of his chair and came slobbering up to us like a big happy dog. He grabbed hold of our hands and pumped them as though he were expecting to get a bucket of water from each of us - and then he led us immediately to the minivans. We hadn't said we were interested in a minivan, mind you - just a van. But John had a lot of minivans on the lot, so that's what he figured we needed.

As he launched into his canned speech about the glories of the American minivan he waved his arms like a frantic Macarena dancer. "We have this one, and this one, and this one, and this one." he said. The Lovely Marianne bobbed and weaved to stay out of his way as he flailed and twirled.

"What about a Club Wagon Chateau?" I asked. "You got any of those?"

He looked at me as though I had just dropped a rat on his cheese cake. "Oh no!" he shrieked. "A Club Wagon *Chateau* goes for big bucks! They're *much* too expensive! *Everyone's* buying minivans nowadays. I have this one, and this one, and this one."

Now, I want to make sure you're following this. John was speaking to two people who had *proven* their ability to both afford and *buy* a Club Wagon Chateau. We drove up in one, right? Parked it right in front of John's plate-glass window. But nevertheless, John took one look at us and decided we simply couldn't afford another one. "They're *much* too expensive!" he said. Isn't that precious?

I told him about the countless hours I spend on the road, motoring from one seminar city to the next. I also told him of the four teenage daughters we had spawned -one now in college, and each with her own posse. "I need to transport more stuff than Mayflower Van Lines," I explained. "On the average day, I drive more people around than Ralph Kramden," I said. But he didn't say, "Well, Dan, I'm *sure* you don't want to give up *any* of the space or luxury you've come to enjoy over the past four years while driving our top-of-the-line van. Let's face it, a minivan would seem *small* to you at this stage in your life. Why, you'd have to remove four of the back seats to fit all that stuff you schlep out to your daughter's school. That means you wouldn't be able to take any of your other daughters with you on those college trips. Hey, suppose you want one of them to see that school next year. How can you do that with just three seats? No, Dan, I think you're *right* to want another Club Wagon Chateau. Tell you what. Let's do some creative financing so you won't have to take a step backwards when it comes to your personal comfort and convenience. Okay?"

He could have said that. In a New York minute he could have shoved us right over the edge.

But noooooo! Instead of giving me what I wanted, and then selling me options, John talked me into a minivan. He was *that* good!

He showed me how I could use the roof rack ("It's exterior space!") and he explained with a wink how I probably didn't *really* want to take all those daughters along ("Hey, more time for you and the wife to be alone. Know what I mean?"). He talked both me and himself right out of that expensive Club Wagon Chateau. Why? Because he decided we couldn't afford one. Even though we already owned one.

Maybe *he* couldn't afford one. But is that reason enough to convince me that I can't afford one either?

The minivan *is* nice, but that's not my point. This goes on all the time in the heating business. Read on.

The Pittsburgh Pessimist

I will never forget this guy because he was so passionate in his belief that people should not be spending too much money with him during a recession. It was 1992, bad times were reigning, and some home owner had just called this plumber to ask about hydronic radiant heat, which had been featured on TV (probably on *This Old House*).

"Do you have a list of reasons why hydronic radiant heat is no good?" he asked me.

I took a minute to let that sink in. You know, I looked around for Alan Funt and the Candid Camera. "What do you mean?" I asked.

"Well, I've got these people who are calling me, wanting to install hydronic radiant heat, like that guy on TV puts in? I don't think it's a good idea because I understand this stuff is expensive."

"It does cost more than other systems, but it also *saves* a lot of money on the operating costs," I said. "Hydronic radiant pays for itself in fuel savings. And then there's the issue of comfort. There's nothing nicer than a warm floor..."

"But," he interrupted, "I don't think anybody should be spending that much money when the country's in trouble like it is right now. Can't you give me a list of reasons I can give to these people to help them change their minds?"

"Are you serious?" I asked.

"Of course I'm serious!"

"Why would you want them to change their minds?"

"Because of the recession. I told you that."

"What does that have to do with these people?" I asked. "Do you really think you should be telling them how to spend their money?"

"I can put in a much cheaper system that will still heat their house," he said.

"But they want *hydronic radiant*. They're telling you that. Now all you have to do is show up and take their money. That will make them feel good, and it will go a long way toward ending your personal recession."

"You know what things cost nowadays?" he said, not hearing a word I had just sputtered. "You know how tough it is trying to make ends meet? You know how hard it is to get a job with this recession going on. Nobody's got any money."

Please believe me when I tell you this is a <u>true</u> story. It happened exactly as I've told it.

And this is your competition, Wet Head. Think you can handle him?

A Connecticut Wholesaler Who Knew Best

Here's another one that sprang from your TV set. At some point, Richard Trethewey installed some radiant baseboard in a home featured on *This Old House*. The product happened to be RadinatPanel from Radiant Technology Inc.

A woman in Connecticut - a place where many rich people live - saw the RadiantPanel and decided this would be perfect for her old house because it doesn't look like a radiator. It disappeared into the architecture, a point Trethewey had made on the TV.

He convinced this rich lady, and now she was trying like crazy to buy some of the stuff.

She called this wholesaler, and he told her that stuff was too expensive, and that she should buy copper fin-tube baseboard instead. He had plenty of this in stock, and he would have to special-order the other stuff. Besides, she would need more of the RadiantPanel because it only puts out about one-third of the BTUs of copper fin-tube baseboard. That's because it works by radiation, not by convection.

The rich lady told the wholesaler that she *really* liked the RadiantPanel and wanted it because of its good looks.

The wholesaler told her she should get the copper fin-tube because he thought it was a better value.

Now, I know this is a true story because I sat over a cup of coffee with this wholesaler while he told it. He was very proud of himself. "That woman was a real moron," he said. "She wanted to spend, like, five times what she had to."

"What did you finally do?" I asked.

"I told her I couldn't help her, and that she should go someplace else."

Which is what she most likely did.

Again, Wet Head, think you can handle the competition? Would you be willing to take the rich woman's money? All you have to do is show up, for Pete's sake.

A Lesson From La La Land

I got a call from a guy in Los Angeles who wanted to have radiant heat installed under his slate patio. When I asked why he would want to install radiant heat under a Los Angeles patio he said, "Because I'm rich, and because I can."

That was good enough for me.

The problem he was having was that he couldn't find a contractor who would do the job. I gave him the phone numbers of three major providers of radiant floor tubing. I figured they'd follow up with names of local contractors capable of doing this sort of basic hydronic work.

Two weeks later, the rich guy wrote to let me know that although he had contacted the three tubing manufacturers, only two contractors had contacted him as a result. One contractor said he was 80 miles away, and not interested in traveling that far for such a small job. The other guy was local, but he said he only did commercial work.

"That's a shame," the rich guy said, "because I made my fortune in commercial real estate and this contractor could have become my main guy, had I liked his work."

Are you paying attention to this? Hard to believe, isn't it? Stand back and watch as the excitement bubbles up from the home owners' end of the business because of TV, the Internet, and all these home-repair magazines that are popping up on the newsstands. Watch the way most contractors handle these people when they call.

All you have to do is pay attention, Wet Head, and be ready to serve. That's all.

Deep In The Heart Of Texas

There was this 75-year-old couple who were building a new house in Hillsboro, Texas, which is 62 miles south of Dallas. They had lived with a certain Weil-McLain boiler for quite a while, and they wanted to take it with them from their old house to their new house. "They're knocking our old house down to build a development," the husband said. "They gave us a price we couldn't refuse, and the boiler's not that old. We plan to live a *lot* longer."

The trouble was they couldn't find a Texas contractor who would install the old boiler in their brand-new, very expensive home. "We tried, but no luck," the wife told me on the phone. "The contractors we talked to said hydronic heat was no good. That it was bad for our health. That it would dry out our furniture."

"What a bunch of idiots!" the old man shouted into my ear. "We've been living with this type of heat for *37 years*, and we don't want to give it up. But we can't find anyone willing to take our money!"

They finally found an engineer in Waco who had grown up in Michigan. He designed the new system. Then they found a willing plumber who had worked in Dallas for years on industrial installations. He put the old boiler and the new piping system in for them.

It shouldn't be this hard for people to spend their money. If you can't make money in this country, you're simply not paying attention.

The Lone Star state needs more Wet Heads.

Anybody paying attention?

And Then There's My $453.85 Ceiling Fan Switch

We once had a dormer put on the top of our house. When the contractor finished with that project we had him move a few walls downstairs. By the time he was through, we knew more about this guy and his crew than we cared to know. We were more than happy to say good-bye and get our lives back to normal.

The last thing we needed to have done (and this was months after the contractor had left) was to have a ceiling fan switch moved from one wall to the other. I wasn't looking for any great talent here. The electrician just needed a license and the right price. That's all. I wasn't looking for any long-term commitments here. I just wanted a switch moved.

I found a local guy who would do it for fifty bucks. "Deal!" I said.

And here's what happened.

"This is a beautiful house!" he said as he worked on the switch.

"Thanks," The Lovely Marianne, said with a big smile. She loves it when people say nice things about her house. "We've been working on it for six months."

"I know," he said, "my wife and I live right here in the neighborhood."

"Oh, you do?" she said.

"We sure do!" He kept working away. "And we've been watching your job as it's been going along. In fact, we drove by just the other night."

"Uh huh," The Lovely Marianne said.

"Yeah, it was dark."

"It gets like that at night," I said.

"No, I mean it was *real* dark. No moon."

"Uh huh," The Lovely Marianne said.

He just kept working away at that ceiling fan switch. "Yeah, my wife mentioned how dark it was on the side of your house," he said finally. "'Boy,' she said to me, 'if I lived there I'd be nervous if you weren't home, Lee.'"

And The Lovely Marianne looked at me. And that look reflected all the terrors of childhood, all the fears that live in the night and visit young women when the husband is AWAY ON BUSINESS. As I so often am.

"Well, what can you do?" she said, shrugging her little shoulders.

"Oh," he said as he continued to tinker with my $50 ceiling fan switch, "I can put in a flood light with a motion detector if you'd like. It's not expensive. Do you travel, Mr. Holohan?"

"Yes," I said, unconsciously grabbing my wallet.

"What do you do?"

"I write, and I lecture."

"Oh, that's great! I've always wanted to be a writer."

"That's nice," I said.

"Do you have a computer, Mr. Holohan?"

I took him into my office and showed him all the neat electronic stuff I have.

"Do you have surge protectors on all this equipment?" he asked in a most helpful way.

"Of course I do," I answered. "Who would have all of this and not have a surge protector?"

He smiled and kept looking at all the expensive equipment. "That's good, very good," he said," Surge protectors will protect you from just about anything."

"What do you mean 'just about'?" I asked.

"Well, they won't help if your house gets hit by lighting, for instance."

"*Nothing* will help if my house gets hit by lightning," I said.

"Oh no, that's not true! I can put a lightning protector in the circuit box. You just *gotta* see these things! They could have put Doctor Frankenstein out of business!" He got all excited about this. He was smiling and waving his arms - tickled pink that he was going to be able to solve a problem I didn't even know I had.

"Can you do that when you're doing the flood lights?" The Lovely Marianne asked from the doorway.

"No problem," Lee said.

And that's how I bought my $453.85 "ceiling fan switch." Lee was *that* good.

He sold me by approaching things from my self-interest. He grabbed my attention by pointing out a few potential problems while he was there in my house doing something else for me. He explained in a friendly way how he had a solution to my potential problems. He never pressured me; he just showed me what was possible. And then he gave me the opportunity to make a decision.

When I got to know him better (he does all our electrical work now) I asked him if he does this to everyone. "Sure!" he said. "It's just my way of being helpful. I like to notice things when I'm in someone's house. I make suggestions, and most of the time people take me up on them because I'm already there."

"Do you ever think that people can't afford the things you suggest?" I asked, remembering a couple of those heating contractors I told you about before. Lee looked at me as if I was making a joke. "If people can't afford it," he said, "they won't buy it." He chuckled. "It's not my job to tell them what they can and can't afford. I just make suggestions and leave that decision up to them."

I like to think of Lee as an electrical Wet Head.

He's *very* successful, by the way.

You Want Fries With That?

I know a contractor who wasn't doing so well. He was an expert at high-end hydronic installations, and his work was masterful. He used nothing but the best equipment, and his mechanics were artists. His only problem was that he was starving to death.

"How's business?" I asked one day when I ran into him at a trade show.

"It stinks," he said. "And I'm *so* frustrated. I offer these people the *best* possible hydronic heating systems, but they always balk at the price."

"Is your price always that high?" I asked.

"It sure is! Hey, I sell nothing but the best!"

"Do you try to talk to the people?"

"Of course I do," he said, "But they get into this 'What if we took this part out?' thing." He shook his head in disgust. "You know what I mean? They'll say, 'What if we took out some of those expensive controls?' That sort of thing. I think my high prices might shake them up so much that, right away, they try to find a way to cut it down."

"What do you do when they try to cut things out of the job?" I asked.

He laughed. "I tell them to *forget* about it! We sell nothing but the best. If they want less than the best, they're dealing with the wrong company. That's it!"

"But couldn't you make the system work with different controls?" I asked.

"Sure, I could," he said. "But then the system wouldn't be as good. We sell only the *best*."

"But you're not actually selling *anything* right now, are you? The best or otherwise."

"That's the problem," he admitted, shaking his head. "If things don't get better soon, we're going to be in big trouble."

Things did get better, but not because he kept doing what he had been doing. They got better because of a lesson he learned from a young kid behind the counter at McDonald's.

"How's business?" I asked when I ran into him a few months later.

"Business is unbelievable!" he gushed. "We've finally discovered the secret of selling high-end-hydronic heating systems."

"And what might that be?" I asked.

"First, you have to present the products in the customer's self-interest," he explained.

"I know that," I said. "Customers need to understand what's in it for them. If they don't, they simply won't buy."

"You got *that* right!" he agreed. "But there's *more* to the selling of high-end hydronics than just that."

"Tell me," I begged, anxious to hear of his revelation.

"It's the *fries*," he explained with a Zen-like smile.

"The fries?"

"Yeah. I went into McDonald's and ordered a Big Mac, right? The kid punches the button on the register, and then says to me, 'You want fries with that?' I said okay, not really thinking about it. Then he says, 'You want something to drink?' I told him to give me a Coke. Then he goes, 'You wanna Super Size your order?' and I said, 'Sure, why not?' Finally, he looks up and asks, 'How about a nice, hot apple pie? They're really fresh right now.' I figured, what the hell. I ordered a hot apple pie."

My friend was sputtering all over himself with excitement by this point.

"So what's your great business revelation?" I asked.

"It's the *fries*! You know, the way the kid asked me if I wanted *fries* with the Big Mac! Don't you get it?" he shouted, not believing that I didn't.

"I don't get it," I admitted.

"The McDonald's people ask what you want, and then they suggest things that would make your desires even *better*." He was smiling like a little kid with a Happy Meal. "We started to do the same thing with our proposals. We'd go in with a good, basic package - one that wasn't outrageously priced - and once the people understood, and agreed to that basic package, we'd ask them if they wanted some fries!"

"French fries?" I asked.

"No, not exactly *fries*, Dan. We'd offer them the hydronic equivalent of fries. You know, things like hydronic towel warmers, warm floors in the kitchen, outdoor reset controls to save money on fuel while increasing their comfort - all the goodies you won't find in the basic system. We'd offer them one thing at a time, and we'd make it all sound delicious."

"So you've been selling backwards?" I asked.

"No, not at all!," he said. "*Before*, we were selling backwards. Now, we're selling forward. *Before*, the customers didn't fully understand what we were selling, and because we were hitting them with the works up front, our price scared the heck out of them.

"*Now*, we take lots of time to make sure our proposals put everything in the customer's self-interest. And once they understand that, we build on that basic package. We're selling more high-end hydronic equipment than *ever* before, and it's all because of that kid at McDonald's."

How about that!

Top Selling With An Emphasis On Value

You don't always have to start with the basics and then add the "fries." Your customers will have a lot to do with your strategy, as my friend Alan Levi, Ace Troubleshooter, proves. Here, in his own words, is how he does it.

"I would say my style of sales is "Top Selling with an emphasis on value." I've trained myself to offer the customer a menu of options, but I always begin with the best that is available in the world of hydronics today. From there, I offer other proposals that are less expensive, but I never give them more than three options in all. I've learned that people love to have a choice, but if they have to choose between too many options, they can become confused and overwhelmed.

"I begin each sale with an extensive question-and-answer session. Only by interviewing the client can I discover their perceived needs and objectives. By listening intently, I often discover needs and objectives they themselves haven't fully realized. I always speak plain-English, rather than speak technically, and I always put my proposal in a "what's in it for you" form. I find that when I focus on benefits rather than the technical aspects I get a much better response from clients.

"Once we've established their needs and goals I'll conduct a thorough investigation of the home or building if it's a retrofit job. If it's new construction, I'll have a heat-loss calculation figured from the architect's plans. I like to get the client to bring the plans to my office because my office doubles as a showroom. By having them there, I get to show them working models of the equipment we're proposing. They quickly become comfortable with the equipment, and the showroom reinforces the client's feeling that they are dealing with people who are expert in what they do. They don't have to take my word for it when I say the equipment provides such a high level of comfort; they can feel it for themselves!

"If I can't get them to come to my showroom, I will use photo albums of past jobs to show them work we have done that is similar to what we're proposing for them. I always begin by showing them photos of the outside of the home or building so they get a sense of perspective. I then show them a photo of the old equipment, a photo of the job in progress, and then the finished project. I hold their attention with visual aids rather than depend on my verbal descriptions alone. I'll also give them a copy of our beautiful, full-color corporate brochure, which also reinforces our professionalism.

"Once we've sized the system, I will give them prices on several strategies and options, based on what I've learned about their objectives and needs. We'll set up a mutually convenient time and place to meet. At that time, I'll give them a very detailed estimate of each of their options and answer any questions they may have. I raise the price objection before they can by saying that I don't expect to be the cheapest, and I won't even try to be. I will, however, be the provider of the best value.

"I think what I'm really selling is my enthusiasm, honesty and professionalism. I find the more enthusiastic, honest and professional I am, the better I do at closing sales. I try to leave my clients with the feeling that we are problem solvers, and that we take tremendous pride in what we do.

"I love to sell high-end hydronics, and I always begin with radiant floor heating. Whenever possible, I will recommend this because it's quiet, highly efficient, flexible, and provided incredible comfortable. It fits into any decor that a decorator or architect can dream up. Clients love it, especially if they come to my showroom and experience it firsthand. Towel warmers are so classy, and they provide that feeling of opulence in a bath. I also offer them maximum control by selling as many zones as I can.

It's wonderful when you can be the master of your own thermostat! I also love indirect domestic hot water heaters with their Thermos-bottle insulation, no chimney hassles, high efficiency and long life. They've proven themselves to be winners in my book. Outside reset controls allow for maximum efficiency when tied into a primary/secondary pumping system, such as the one we have in our showroom. I also like high-efficiency, Scotch-marine, cast-iron boilers. They are so well constructed, and they have a certain snob appeal.

"I focus on finding and testing superior hydronic products and ideas because that's our niche. It's what I sold two friends who recently built houses next to each other. These homes are in one of the most exclusive areas of Long Island. One friend chose to spend about $35,000 on her heating system. Her friend was so impressed with the results that she spent $40,000 on her system. These are totally different homes, and the two families had different needs and objectives. We met them both with different solutions, and closed two very nice jobs!"

Wet Head marketers know how to adapt their approach to their individual markets. This comes from knowing who their customers are, and then approaching them in their self-interest.

You can do this too.

Truckin'

Dennis Bellanti is one of my favorite Wet Heads because he is so unbelievably positive about everything he does. Dennis runs a wholesale distributorship in Englewood, CO that goes by the name Low Energy

Systems. He drives around his territory pulling a trailer containing a boiler, radiators, and a radiant heating system. The back of the trailer had one of those red circles with the diagonal line, like a No Smoking sign. Inside Dennis' red circle are the words Scorched Air. He says scorched air guys often flip him the bird.

You gotta love this guy.

He takes his trailer out on the road to show contractors and home owners the glories of hydronic heat. He lets them feel the comfort, and because he does, he is very successful.

He distinguishes himself from his competitors. He is passionate. He is creative because he puts the things he sees around him together to form new combinations. He is also having a lot of fun.

Recently, Dennis wrote me a letter and I asked if I could share part of it with you. I think you'll benefit by from what Dennis has to say.

"Teaming up with a good customer, I recently sold a ski area on the idea of hydronic radiant heat. They currently had a scorched air system and were going to do an addition and remodel the lodge. One problem area was the boot rental room. You see, when the boots come back they are snow-packed and wet. In the past, the management relied on some extra scorched air ducts in that room to dry the boots and remove the humidity. My solution was to offer them a heat-recovery ventilator with a de-humidistat to not only remove the excess humidity, but also to remove smoke from the lounge. This not only added several thousand dollars to the sale, it also made a happy customer.

"There is no justification in my mind for scorched air heat or even a combination system. Most people will buy a hot water system when you give them a reason to do so. The ones that don't, deserve to be unhealthy and uncomfortable.

"It all comes down to quality, one-on-one selling. I think that a contractor who is armed with knowledge, enthusiasm and dedication to his profession can do wonders. He or she doesn't have to take the Zig Ziglar sales course (although it would help). Take this enthused, hard-working person, arm them with quality literature and let them go head-to-head with the scorched air guy. Every time the Wet Head offers a reason to buy his system, the Air Head can only say, 'But mine's cheaper.'

"Now, as a last thought on successful hydronic marketing, how about this? I was zipping down the highway after a long day visiting customers. Windshield time makes my mind work in strange ways. I passed a truck dealership where they were selling retired rental box vans. It gave me this crazy idea. What would happen if an enthusiastic contractor bought one of the high-mileage vans for say, $5,000? Then he slapped a cheap paint job on it for another $1,000. After that, he would call his favorite suppliers and manufacturers and propose this: I've got this van that I'm going to use to promote your products. I will put one of your small boilers in it and I'm going to hang some cool radiators on the wall with maybe a heated towel rack. And then I will take some scraps from my shop and put radiant floor heat in it. I will then take it to home shows to let people feel the comfort. I'll even take it to a customer's house when they ask me for a bid on a new heating system. I'll let them feel the comfort, too! All I ask is that you provide me with some of the materials I need. Use my co-op funds.

"So now, Dan, for about $8,000 in materials and a few evenings and weekends this contractor could have the hottest showroom around."

See? You don't have to spend a fortune. You just have to be enthusiastic like Dennis.

Life is short. Why be dull?

Our Specials Today Are . . .

Alan Levi, Dennis Ballanti and other smart Wet Heads have learned the lesson restaurant owners have been trying to teach us for years. Give the customer a menu, talk about the specials of the day, and ask if they'd like something to drink. Then offer dessert.

Lay out the options. Don't decide what the customer wants before you offer the menu.

The other day I went into a restaurant and the waiter said to me, "You look like a hamburger guy to me."

"I'd really like to see a menu," I said.

"Nope," he answered, "you're a hamburger guy."

"Don't you have a menu?" I asked.

"Sure we do," he said. "But there's a lot of expensive food on that menu, and from the looks of you, I don't think you can afford any of it so I'm not even going to show it to you. Let me bring you a nice greasy hamburger, okay?"

I'm kidding. That didn't really happen.

Things like that never happen in restaurants.

They only happen when heating contractors start to believe that just because *they* can't afford it, *no one* can afford it. "Let me give you the cheapest system I can build," they say, "I know you're only interested in price."

These guys have yet to discover the Principle of the Menu - even though it's all around them.

Your customers are old enough to make up their own minds. Hand them a menu.

Competence

A woman came to a steam seminar we sponsored in Pennsylvania not long ago. During a break, I asked what she did for a living. "I'm not in the business," she said. I asked her why she would come to a steam heating seminar if she wasn't in the business and she told me she owned a steam-heated apartment building. "I can't find a contractor who is capable of saving me fuel. I feel like I've been talking to people who don't know what they're doing. They take my money, but they don't save me any fuel. I've given up on them."

"What are you looking for in a heating contractor?" I asked.

"Competence," she said.

I thought about what a sad commentary that was. I mentioned what she had said to the group when we got back together after the break. The smart contractors descended on her like fighter jets during the next break. Wet

Heads will always find opportunity when other contractors choose to be incompetent.

Now, if you cornered this woman and started talking about a boiler's impressive AFUE, she might start nodding her head at you (remember the Hinge Principle?). This woman's not in the market for a new boiler. She's in the market for lower fuel bills. She told me that. The contractor who addresses that need will be the one she considers competent.

I write for a magazine called *Old-House Journal*. This magazine has nothing to do with the TV show, *This Old House*; this magazine has been around *much* longer than that TV show. People who restore old houses read this magazine and they like meaty articles filled with technical substance. Whenever I write an article for *OHJ* I always receive hundreds of phone calls, faxes and letters from readers. In just almost every cases, the reader asks me if I can recommend a heating contractor in their area who is competent.

They never ask for the cheapest heating contractor.

They never ask for the fastest heating contractor.

They never ask for the best-looking heating contractor.

They just ask for one who is competent. You see, you don't have to be perfect; you just have to be competent because in the Land of the Blind, the one-eyed man is king.

I once met a salesman who worked for a heating company. He prided himself on being able to give a home owner a price on a replacement steam boiler without visiting the house. "How can you possibly do that?" I asked. "I just have them read me the data off the old name plate," he said. "Then I quote a replacement. It's telemarketing!"

"There's a lot more involved when you're changing a steam boiler than what's written on the label," I cautioned him.

"Maybe so," he said, "but that's for the guys in the field to work out. My job is to get the order. Nothing happens until you get the order."

"Maybe so," I said, "but I'd still want to get a look at that old system before I gave the people a price." He told me he didn't have time to go traipsing around the field looking at old systems. Truth was, this guy never went out in the field to do, or even *watch*, the actual work. In fact, he looked down on the guys in his company who *did* do the work. "Wrench Jockeys," he called them.

You can compete with this guy, can't you? You just have to be competent.

Keep focusing on that.

Don't Lose Sight Of The Intangibles

There's a karate school in the next town that runs an ad in the local PENNYSAVER. The ad doesn't say, Bring us your child and within six months we will have her kicking the snot out of all the bullies in school. Rather, it says, "We will teach your child confidence, self-esteem, self-discipline, and self-defense. Your child will have better grades in school, and will be able to avoid peer pressure and the temptation of drugs."

How's that for selling intangibles?

Sort of reminds you of what the Quiet May folks were doing during the 1930s, doesn't it? They weren't selling oil burners; they were selling health, cleanliness, time, family togetherness, peace of mind, love and friendship.

I was walking through the mall the other day when I came upon one of those photo booths. I'm sure you've seen these too. You sit inside, draw the curtains, adjust the seat, stick in a couple of bucks and smile. The photo comes out in a minute or two and you save it in your sock drawer for years.

You know what it said on the outside of this booth?

INSTANT MEMORIES.

Now, I don't know about you but I think that's positively wonderful. Polaroid isn't selling photographs; they're selling instant memories. How deliciously intangible is that?

None of this is new news, though. Human beings have been buying intangibles for as long as anyone can remember.

Eve didn't buy that apple because she was hungry.

Delight Your Customers!

When you finally get that order for your next hydronic system, take a minute to think about what the customer expects from you. Once you've decided what that is, delight them by doing something more than they expected.

There's a magic to this. Every human being in the world loves to get something for nothing.

I used to know this guy who owned a candy store in a big mall here on Long Island. It was one of those places where you order lose candy in whatever quantity your sweet tooth demands.

"Gimme a pound of gummy bears," a customer would say to the perky young blond woman behind the counter. She'd smile and shove her stainless-steel scoop deep down into this huge plastic tub of gummy bears. Then she'd jiggle them onto the scale.

This went on day in and day out.

The guy who owned the store employed four young women. Two worked during the day; the other two handled the night shift. One day the owner noticed that most of his daytime customers were buying from just one of these young women. Her name was Mary.

People would wait a long time on line for Mary, even though Sally, the other young woman, was more than willing to help them.

"May I help the next person on line?" Sally would say.

"That's all right," the next person on line would answer, "I'll wait for her." Then he'd point at Mary, who would smile like the queen of the prom.

This went on day in and day out but Sally was pretty good-natured about it. She'd continually ask people if she could help them, but they'd almost always refuse. So she'd clean up the counter and wait on the occasional people who had not frequented the candy store before and who *would* let her help them.

This seemed incredibly strange to the owner and, being a Long Islander, he immediately suspected the worst.

"Mary's robbing me blind!" he whispered to me one day.

"No!" I said in astonishment. "Mary? How do you know?"

"Everyone *waits* for her," he said with annoyance. "Sally's standing there, offering to help, but they all want Mary. She's *got* to be giving them more than they're paying for. So much of my business comes from people who are regulars. She's *got to* be giving it away."

"Are you noticing any candy missing?" I asked.

"Ahh, it's hard to say in this business," he said. "Most of the time I don't know what the heck's going on."

"So what are you going to do about Mary?" I asked.

"I'd like to fire her," he said, "but I really don't have any grounds other than my suspicions. I'm not looking to get into trouble with the Labor Board, and besides, she's a pretty good worker - except for the stealing, that is."

"Which you're not even sure she's doing," I added.

"Well, if she's *not* stealing," he reasoned, as any true Long Islander would, "why the heck is everyone waiting for her?"

"Beats me," I said.

The guy became obsessed with Mary. He'd watch her out of the corner of his eye all day long, but he could never catch her doing anything other than taking care of just about every customer who walked through the door.

Finally, with his obsession rising to new heights, he hired a private detective to watch her. He figured the detective would get the goods on Mary once and for all. And then he could fire her.

The detective sat on a bench outside the store for a week and watched everything that went on. He billed the owner $800.00 a day for this service.

Finally, at the end of the week, the detective issued a short report to the owner. The report explained, once and for all, why everyone was going to Mary and not to Sally. When I read that short report, my first thought was that this detective was brilliant, and that he was worth every dollar he charged my friend.

My second thought was that Mary was even *more* brilliant, but I'll bet she didn't even realize what she was doing.

Here's what was going on: When a customer asked Mary for a pound of gummy bears, she would smile and stick that stainless-steel scoop of hers into the bin. A second later, she'd come up with about three-quarters of a pound of gummy bears. Then she'd slowly jiggle the entire scoop onto the scale as the customer watched. She'd smile at the customer and then return to the bin for more gummy bears. These, too, she'd jiggle onto the scale. She did this slowly, maybe two gummy bears at a time. All the while, she'd smile and giggle as the customer watched, his tongue hanging out of his mouth with desire. It was really something to see.

When Mary reached the pound mark on the scale, she immediately stopped jiggling. Not one additional gummy bear fell onto that scale once the pound mark had been reached. Mary would then pour the candy into a plastic bag, close it with a twist-tie, hand it to the now-nearly-berserk customer, giggle the most wondrous giggle you have ever heard and say, "Hope you like 'em!"

The customer would rip into that bag like a starving raccoon and stuff a handful into his mouth.

"Mmmmmppph," he would say with a smile.

This went on day in and day out.

Sally, on the other hand, handled things differently.

"Gimme a pound of gummy bears," a customer who had never before visited the store would say to Sally.

Sally, happy to be doing something, would jam the stainless-steel scoop elbow-deep into the gummy bear bin and then slam-dunk about a pound-and-a-quarter of candy onto the scale.

"I said a *pound*," the customer would sneer, as only a Long Islander can.

"I *know* what you said," Sally would answer back in an equally surly voice.

And then she'd do the most maddening thing. She'd remove the gummy bears from the scale in little scoops. Little by little she'd take gummy bears away until the scale read exactly one pound. Then she'd pour them into a bag, twist tie them and hand them to the customer who, at this point, seemed reluctant to accept them. He felt somehow cheated.

According to the detective's report, the customers waited for Mary simply because Sally had this habit of putting too many gummy bears on the scale. You see, once those bears went on that scale the customers felt they owned them. And as soon as Sally began to take them back, she was nothing more than a lousy thief.

This was the reason why no one went to Sally more than once.

Mary gave them more than they expected - even though it was the same amount.

Something For Nothing?

True story: In New York City, there exists a grand and glorious place called the Jewish delicatessen. You order your sandwich at the tall metal-and-glass counter, and then watch with watering mouth as some guy named Moe slices pastrami-to-die-for and lays it tenderly onto the freshest seeded rye bread in the world.

At some point in this process, Moe looks around for the boss, and not seeing him, he hands you over the counter a juicy slice of that wonderful pastrami. Moe has a look of larceny and conspiracy in his eyes as he does this. You quickly take the pastrami from his hand, as he holds the index finger of his other hand up to his pursed lips. "Shhhhhh," he whispers.

You nod, joining the conspiracy against the owner, knowing in your heart you just got something for nothing. You bite down. This is the most delicious slice of pastrami you have ever tasted in your life. Moe smiles. "Good?" he mouths silently. You nod. And then, after looking again for the boss, he hands another piece of this heavenly meat over the counter. You're in deli heaven.

Good ol' Moe!, you think. What a guy. He wraps your sandwich in white deli paper, hands it to you, and you give him a dollar tip. He winks at you, the conspiracy complete. Good ol' Moe!

You smile to yourself as walk to your table. You savor that last "free" slice of pastrami before swallowing. You lick your lips while thinking about how swell Moe is.

In reality, Moe gave you two slices of pastrami that were going to wind up on your sandwich anyway, had you not taken them from his pudgy hand. You just *thought* you got something for nothing. Moe gave you squat.

So how come it felt so good? And why are you going to go back to Moe's deli at the first possible chance.

Seventy years ago, Claude C. Hopkins wrote in his book, *Scientific Advertising*, "Remember that the people you address are selfish, as we all are." There's not a regular human being in the world who doesn't want to get something for nothing.

Or at least *think* he got something for nothing.

Free Thermostats?

I met a heating contractor who gives the customer a "free" thermostat every time he does a boiler job. He just pops up in the middle of the job with a smile that could light up a gymnasium and declares, "Say, you know what? Now that you have this beautiful new boiler that's going to keep you warm for years to come I think you should also have a new clock thermostat to go along with it. Tell you what. I'm gonna put one in at no extra charge, as my way of saying thanks for your business. How would that be with you?"

Now he charges them for the thermostat, of course. It's in his price from the git-go. But when he *gives* it to them, he tells me the customers smile like they just won the lottery. Then they tell their neighbors all about the great deal, and the contractor keeps getting more and more boiler jobs.

He's been doing this for years.

"You know what most home owners think of when they consider their heating systems, Dan?" he asked me once.

"What?" I said.

"They think of the *thermostat*," he said, with a big satisfied grin. "That's why I give 'em away, Dan! Makes the folks feel real good. And then because most folks can't program these things, I do it for them. It ask them to write down how they come and go from day to day. You know, when they go to bed, when they wake up, what time they leave for work. I want to make sure I adjust the temperature of that house to best fit their life style.

"Then I explain that once I program the thermostat, I'll keep that activity list in my office vault. That way, should there be a power failure, and if the battery in the thermostat doesn't work, I'll be able to reset the thermostat exactly as it was before. No charge for the service, should you ever need it."

Is it any wonder people tell their friends about this guy?

Back To The Deli For A Moment

How many times have you gone to the deli counter in your local supermarket to order a pound of turkey or ham or whatever and the clerk says, "It's a little over. Is that all right?"

If you're like me, you'll say, "Yeah, that's all right."

How much extra turkey or ham or whatever do you suppose you could move in a year by giving every customer "a little bit over." Most people accept the extras when offered. They figure, what the heck, they've decided to make the purchase already. So if they get a little bit more, that only means they won't have to come back again so soon.

When you think about it, it's actually a convenience for the customer.

Suppose you were to offer "a little bit over" on every job you did. Offer it while you're doing the job. "You know, as long as I'm here I could also do this for you. And I can give you a special price because I'm already here. That will save you money."

It can't hurt to ask, can it?

It works for the deli guy, and it can work for you too.

Valve Tags

Frank Blau, my colleague at *Plumbing & Mechanical* magazine, came up with an idea that has done a lot of good for a lot of people. His company specializes in "sudden service," and he realized long ago that many home owners don't know what to do in a mechanical emergency. Now, Frank is the sort of guy who will always turn a problem into a business, so once he recognized the home owner's dilemma, he decided to do something about it.

He had a printer make some day-glow orange tags out of cardboard. On one side is his business card, and on the other side is a list of common valves and switches found in everyone's home. Next to each item is a small box, which a technician can punch like a train ticket. Frank had the cards laminated in plastic, and he attached a loop to each.

Frank has his service technicians attach these tags to the valves and switches when they visit a home to do service work.. He even manages to get paid for this service, because the tags have a value to the home owner. In an emergency, the home owner will know what operates what.

The best part is when Frank's guy is done, the plumbing and heating equipment looks like a Christmas tree with all those day-glow orange tags. And every one of those tags has Frank's name and phone number on it.

Frank was so successful with the valve tag idea that he decided to sell the tags to other contractors. He now pays handicapped people to make the tags, which he sells all over the country. Everyone wins.

See? There are no problems; there are only opportunities.

Things Remembered

I once met a contractor who installed a lot of boilers. When he was finished with each, he would polish the jacket with car wax. He'd also paint the pipes. Then he would affix a brass plate to the front of the boiler. He bought these brass name plates a store in the mall called Things Remembered. On each brass name plate he would have them engrave his company's name and the words, "This boiler was proudly installed by (the installer's name)."

It may seem like a silly thing, and he certainly didn't have to do this, but that little brass tag did wonders for his business. And the installer stood a bit taller every time he finished a job. Like a proud artist, he got to sign his work. Nice touch, isn't it?

You can get these brass plates made for next to nothing, and the price disappears in the boiler job. When you stick one on a boiler you will be doing something that hardly *anyone* else does anymore - you will be signing your work. And no service company that visits that job in the years to come will dare put a sticker over your name plate.

You see? You don't have to spend a fortune to stand out and be remembered.

Don't Kick The Bucket

Speaking of stickers, I've been on jobs where the paper stickers extend about three

inches off the boiler. Every service company that visits puts their sticker over the last guy's sticker.

I know a fuel oil dealer in New York City who gets around this, though. He doesn't use stickers; he uses buckets. He puts one under *every* low-water cutoff on *every* steam boiler he services (lots of steam heat in New York City!). The bucket replaces the sticker because it has his company's name and phone number on it. And since the customer has to blow-down the low-water cutoff once a week, he can't get away from the name of his oil dealer. He carries the name to the drain and reads it off the side of the bucket as he dumps the dirty water.

This is absolutely brilliant because let's say a customer gets tempted away by a low price from a competing oil dealer. My guy is out of luck, right? Wrong! The new guy can't possibly offer the level of service my guy offers because the new guy's price is too low. Before long, the customer will get disgusted with the new guy and long for my guy.

He'll remember my guy because once a week, he sees that name on the bucket. He remembers all that great service. And the new guy could never afford to give him a bucket. His price is too low!

It may take a little while, but that bucket gets those customers back.

(Did you know some thermostat manufacturers will put your company name on the thermostat? Something to think about, eh?)

Quote With Lots Of Paper

A contractor friend told me he increased his business by fifty percent in one year by just making this one change to the way he was doing business. I had mentioned the technique of quoting with a lot of paper at a seminar and he had taken it to heart. It worked very well for him.

Here's what I mean by using a lot of paper. When a home owner considers a purchase as major as a new hydronic heating system, or even just a replacement boiler, she'll probably get at least three quotes on the job, right? Now, consider what most contractors' quotes look like. They're on a single page, and the contractor will often use a rubber stamp to imprint his letterhead. The quote is filled with misspelled words. The paper had smudges all over it; you'll sometimes see coffee stains and cigarette burns as well. The quote might read, "We will supply and install a new boiler and controls." Then there's a price. The contractor will often leave out the model number because he doesn't want the home owner to get another quote on the same boiler, or worse, check the price of the boiler at The Home Depot.

The home owner looks at this quote and doesn't learn much, right?

Now, here's what you can do to stand out. Get all the literature you can from the manufacturers you regularly use and dig the *benefits* out of that literature - not the features, the *benefits*. For instance, Slant/Fin just sent me some literature on a new boiler. One of the features they list is Sealed Combustion. What's that mean to a home owner? Not much, right? But right after they see Sealed Combustion, they say,

"Concept 21's combustion process is isolated from the air in your home. Ordinary natural draft boilers typically draw in 20 cubic feet of warmed indoor air per minute, replacing it in your home with cold outside air, which requires extra fuel to heat."

That's a benefit. Sealed Combustion is a feature. See the difference? You could further refine Slant/Fin's description for the home owner by saying it more simply. Like this.

"Everyone knows you can't make a fire without air. Most boilers use the warm air that's already inside your house to make the fire. That means new (much colder!) air has to come in from the outside to replace the warm air the boiler is using. This explains the drafts you feel around windows and electrical outlets. Those drafts are not only uncomfortable, they also waste fuel. The boiler we're going to install in your home is different, though. It gets all its air through a special tube that reaches outdoors like a diver's snorkel. The warmed air in your home stays in your home and you save money."

Work your way through the products you regularly use and come up with these benefits. Most of the time they're right there in the literature. You only have to do this once because you'll keep these benefits in a computer file and spit them out every time you quote a job. That's how you get a meaty quote that's directed right at the customer's self-interest.

Put it all together in a neat pile and use a clear plastic cover, which you'll get at the office supply store. When you present your quote it's going to look so good next to those single-page, dog-eared, coffee-stained, cigarette-burned quotes of your competitors. You'll see a difference in business right away. Remember my contractor friend increased his business by <u>fifty percent</u> in one year by making this one simple change.

Is it worth the effort?

You tell me.

Square BTUs

Never do this.

I met a contractor who used to quote every job at least twenty percent higher than any competitor. "It's because I like to make money," he revealed during a weak moment.

"How do you get the premium price?" I asked.

"I sell only square BTUs," he explained.

"Huh?"

"Yeah, square BTUs," he repeated.

I didn't know what the heck he was talking about so I asked him to elaborate. He took out a piece of white paper and drew this.

"You see, Dan, in the old days builders used to use these round boilers. They called them vertical, fire-tube boilers and they were pretty cheap. 'Builders' specials,' I always called them."

"I'm familiar with them," I said.

"Well, as you can see, when you put a round BTU in a round boiler everything is perfectly fine. Round boiler, round BTUs."

"Huh?" I said, yet again.

"Yes, round BTUs."

"Wait a minute," I said. "BTUs have no shape."

He smiled at me they way you'd smile at a confused child. "Of course a BTU has a shape, Dan. It can be either round or square. And the square ones are the only ones we use. That's why our price will always be higher than the competition." He drew this for me.

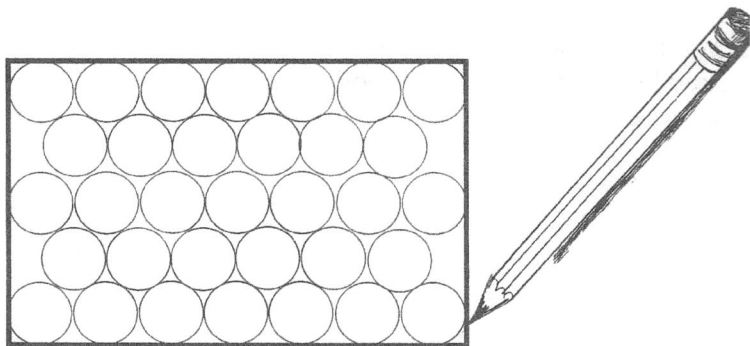

"Now, Dan, as you know, most of the boilers made today are square, not round. And as you can see, when you put round BTUs in a square boiler, you're left with all of these spaces between the BTUs." He pointed to the spaces with the tip of his pencil. "That leads to inefficiency." He smiled at me. I just groaned.

He made another sketch.

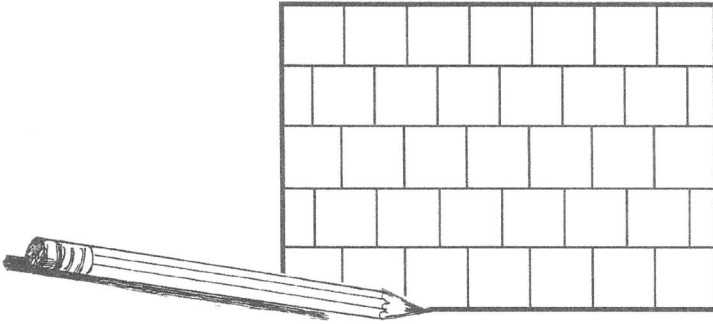

"But when you put *square* BTUs in a *square* boiler, why, those babies fit right up against one another, leaving no gaps, and that, of course, leads to higher efficiency." He gave me a look you could pour on a pancake. "And that's why our price is higher, son."

Now, promise me you'll *never* do this.

11

Getting Noticed

Make Yourself An Expert

Richard Trethewey is probably the best-known heating contractor in America because he is on the PBS series, *This Old House*. Way back when, before *This Old House* became **This Old House**, the producers called Richard's family business and asked his dad if he would go on TV to explain a few things to the viewers. Richard's dad was a bit shy so he suggested they use his son instead. Richard, fortunately, is *not* shy.

The show went on to become a classic, and had Richard decided to grow a beard and wear flannel, he might have became as famous as Norm. Who knows?

He became famous enough, though. I remember walking through Midway airport in Chicago with him once. People kept stopping to stare. "You're *somebody*, right?"

"Right!" Richard would say, as he kept right on walking.

Now, an opportunity such as being a regular on *This Old House* doesn't come along every day, but that's not to say you can't create your own opportunity. I've never been on TV, but I've been on the radio a number of times. People who have these home-repair shows have called me up and had me on as a guest. I've done this live in the studio, and I've also done it through cross-country phone hook-ups. I've always managed to sell some books by being on the radio - and I had fun!

I'm telling you this because there's a good chance that someone in your area is doing a home-improvement show on a local radio station. If you called and told them a bit about yourself - how excited you are about what you're doing, how you're a devoted Wet Head, how you're in the business of keeping babies warm - they just may invite you to be on the radio. They may even make you a regular. And who knows where that might lead?

Have you ever listened to those two guys from Boston who do *Car Talk* on National Public Radio? Just a couple of regular guys, right?

Hey, you never know.

And if you were "the guy on the radio" I'll bet people would want you to install hydronic heating equipment in their homes. What do you think?

How To Get Into A Trade Magazine

If you can get yourself or your company into a trade magazine you'll gain the recognition of your peers. If you're smart, you'll then use that recognition to gain new business. You'll feature the article in your advertising and in your presentations. You'll have reprints made and you'll pass them around to everyone you meet.

This is one of the ways you can become the local expert.

I write articles for seven magazines: *Fueloil & Oil Heat* (read by oil dealers), *Supply House Times* (wholesalers), *Plumbing & Mechanical* (contractors), *PM/Engineer* (engineers), *Contractor* (contractors), *Heating-Plumbing-Air Conditioning* (Canadian contractors), and *Old-House Journal* (home owners). The deadlines for these magazines hit me like waves on a beach and none of the editors is interested in hearing about how busy I am. They just want me to deliver the goods so I'm constantly on the lookout for things to write about. Often, I'll tell a contractor's story in one of my columns. I do this because the contractor took the time to get in touch with me in the right way.

Here's what I mean by the "right way."

One day a contractor called me. "You should write an article about my company," he said.

"Why?"

"Because we're the best in town!"

"What makes you the best?" I asked.

"Well, we just finished a really big job and everything worked."

"Was there anything special about this job?"

"Not really. It was pretty straightforward - no different from the work we usually do. We do good work all the time."

"Did you have to overcome any unusual obstacles to get the job done?" I asked.

"Not really," he said.

"Was the project of historical significance? Did you use any unusual techniques to close the sale? Is there a human interest side to the story? Was the job at the South Pole? Did you have to fight with the natives to get on the site? Do you have twelve toes? Help me out here, willya?"

"I don't think I can. It was just a regular job," he said.

"Then why should I write about it?" I asked.

"Because you wrote about that other guy," he said. "I just think it's our turn."

This is not the "right way" to get into a trade magazine.

Try this instead. Approach me or any other magazine writer or editor in the same way you would approach a prospective customer. Figure out what you do that no one else is doing. Get excited about it, and then tell us your story. Do this, and I guarantee you will be irresistible.

Here's a classic case. A few years ago, Heather McCune, who was then the editor at *Plumbing & Mechanical*, traveled to Colorado to write a story called "Radiant in the Rockies." It was a good story with lots of gorgeous color photos of houses anyone in their right mind would move into tomorrow. The article appeared and we thought that was that.

But then Heather gets this phone call from a guy named Elwin Maurer who proceeds to tell her that he has a different way to doing radiant heat - a way that breaks the mold - and if she knows what's good for her, she'll get back on the plane to see what she missed.

Who could pass this by?

We didn't know if the guy was nuts or what, but he was unbelievably excited and enthusiastic. We couldn't resist.

By the time we got around to doing the story, Heather had moved on to become Chief Editor at *Supply House Times*. Jim Olsztynski and I covered the story and it raised a few of the readers' eyebrows when it appeared. Elwin Maurer put some spark into the magazine. He started a bit of a controversy, which is always fun. It gets people talking to each other.

If you approach the writer or the editor *with something that will be of interest to the readers*, chances are you will get into the magazine. As I said, I write for seven magazines. I began writing for each with a letter that explained who I was and why I thought what I had to say would be of interest to the readers and the advertisers (they're pretty important, those advertisers!). I presented what I had to offer in a way that was in the "customer's" (in this case, the editor's) self-interest.

Sound familiar?

Once you get into a magazine, get reprints made and send them to your local newspaper. Go through the same procedure with them.

Good morning!

Here's an unusual story that I think will be of great interest to your readers. Our company was just featured in this national magazine (I've attached a copy of the story). As you can see it was a local job and it was (usually difficult to do under the circumstances, of historical significance, required savvy engineering skills, the first of its kind in the state, or whatever). I'd be pleased to tell you the story first-hand if you'd like. I'm sure your readers will be as fascinated by what happened here as the readers of the national magazine were. Here's why . . .

Get it? Direct your letter at the editor's self-interest. What's in it for *her*?

Once you get into the newspaper, offer your services to the writer or the editor as a technical advisor for any heating questions that may pop up in the future. Start sending them notes whenever you finish an interesting job. Always present whatever you send in a way that is in their self-interest. Newspaper writers are always looking for interesting "filler" stories to complete an issue. They will appreciate your input tremendously if you don't badger them with phone calls asking when the article will appear. Remember, you want to *help* them, not add to the stress they're already feeling.

Here's something that's guaranteed to get you noticed by editors.

Original Research

Believe it or not, you are in a position to do original research, and newspaper editors love this because it gives them something exclusive. All you have to do is start collecting information from your customers. For instance:

- How oversized is the "average" boiler?

- What is the most-common heating service call?

- How many zones does the "typical" home have?

- What is the most-often-heard complaint about comfort?

- Are people with hydronic heat more comfortable than people with furnaces?

- How long do direct-fired water heaters last in this town?

- How many people have been asking about hydronic radiant heat lately?

- How many people say they are influenced by shows such as *This Old House*?

- How old are the boilers in this town? How about the furnaces?

I'm sure you could come up with a dozen more questions such as these (I came up with this short list by spending five minutes drawing a cluster). The answers will be as interesting to you as they will be to a newspaper editor. These answers can also help you put together a *very* effective advertising campaign and make you look far smarter than your competitors.

And all you have to do is ask questions during or after the job, and keep track of what the folks have to say.

You can do that, can't you? Sure you can!

How About Your Local Library?

As I mentioned, a few years ago The Lovely Marianne and I decided to double the size of our house because the daughters were growing like corn. We wanted to get as much information as we could about general contractors so we got books and asked lots of questions. One day we received a newsletter from the public library. It contained a notice saying that they were going to have a guest speaker talking on the topic, "How to hire a general contractor." We signed up right away.

About 35 people showed up for the talk, which turned out to be very informative. It was given by a local general contractor, by the way. He gave us great insight into general contracting from a home owner's point of view. He also passed out a valuable list of questions we should ask prospective contractors.

He never once plugged his own company, but by the end of his talk everyone in that room asked for his business card.

Think of the possibilities!

- How you can take charge of your old heating system?

- What I learned on my trip to Europe. A better way to heat your home?

- How your hydronic heating system works (and how to get the most from it).

Make yourself and your special knowledge available to your community and watch how quickly they begin to see you as the local expert.

Guess What? Builders Have Competitors

If you decide that builders are cheap, and all they care about is the bottom line, you will be right. However, if you decide that builders are business people who have competitors and are always looking for an edge, you will *also* be right.

The choice is yours. Your attitude will determine your altitude.

Anyone who has ever experienced the joys of hydronic heating knows it delivers glorious comfort. This can be a powerful tool for a builder who is looking to make a distinction between himself and his competitor. Feeling is believing, and when people are looking for a new home, they depend on all five senses to tell them what to do.

This is why builders will light the gas log in the fireplace.

It's why they'll bake bread in the oven.

It's why they'll decorate the rooms with pleasing colors. They want to appeal to all five of the buyer's senses.

As a Wet Head, you can provide that all-over sensation of warmth with hydronics, but you have to be able to get your message across to the builder. This is why it's important for you to have some sort of showroom or display where they can feel hydronic comfort.

Will it cost more? Yes. Will people pay more? Yes, if it's presented in their self-interest. And since hydronics operates at a lower cost, the fuel savings will pay for the system over the life of the mortgage. You have everything going in your favor, but you first have to convince the builder that you can help him sell more of his homes.

So you work with just one builder in your town, becoming his "partner" in business. Perhaps you give him a discount on a hydronic radiant heating system you'll install in his first model home. You're willing to take a risk because the potential rewards are great. You work with the equipment manufacturers to put together a promotional package aimed at home owners. You volunteer to answer any questions potential buyers may have about the heating systems you install.

You show this builder how you can help him sell more homes and he will do business with you. It's a win/win situation, one any smart business person will jump at.

Try it; you'll see what I mean.

Realtors Have Competitors Too

Get in touch with a realtor in your town and offer your technical assistance. When they're selling an older home a realtor will be asked questions about the age or condition of a heating system. It gives them an edge if they can answer these questions. You can help them look good by offering to explain the ins and outs of these systems. If you help the realtor sell homes, they'll send business your way.

Suppose you were to prepare a plain-English booklet showing how different heating systems work, what the advantages and disadvantages are, how they can be improved with zoning, hydronic towel warmers, outdoor-reset, and such. Suppose you gave these booklets to the realtor you're working with to use as a tool. Your name is on the booklet, of course.

Or how about this? Suppose you offered to hold a few training sessions for the realtor's sales people. You'd show them ways to explain how heating systems work to their prospective buyers. As with the builder, you become their "partner" in business, and they reciprocate by giving you leads once they sell the homes.

Don't Neglect ASHI

The American Society of Home Inspectors is an international organization of people who inspect homes for potential buyers. I've spoken to groups of ASHI members across the US and Canada. I once spoke to about 500 of their members in Phoenix at a convention. This is one *very* big association.

If you've never heard of ASHI, call information and get the phone number of their local chapter. Groups of inspectors meet regularly, and they like to hear from knowledgeable speakers. Volunteer to speak at one of their meetings about heating systems, and offer your technical advice to the members over the phone.

When an ASHI inspector is looking over a home for a prospective buyer, and the buyer asks for a recommendation of a local heating contractor who knows his stuff, chances are your name will come up.

Get More Business From Your Existing Customers With A Newsletter

Newsletters can be a very effective way of getting additional business from your existing customers. You worked hard to make these people customers in the first place, and that's why you should stay in touch with them regularly.

To do that well, you'll need to have a list of their names. Ideally, you have this in a computer database.

When you get your mailing list, you'll have to write something for these folks. It doesn't have to be that involved, but it should follow a recipe. Smart Wet Heads follow a classic newsletter recipe that goes like this:

1. **You have a problem.**

2. **Here's what it is.**

3. **Here's what's *causing* that problem.**

4. **Here's how my product or service can solve that problem for you once and for all.**

Alan Levi, Ace Troubleshooter, produces a beautiful newsletter he calls *House Warmers*. He works with a local graphic-design printer to produce and mail it, and he mails it to his residential customers about six times a year. A graphic-design printer is different from the quick-copy guy on the corner. Graphic-design shops have artists on staff. They can take your ideas and turn them into finished products. Some graphic-design printers will also handle the bulk mailing for you.

A good graphic-design printer can do you almost as much good as an advertising agency.

I'd like to share a story from a recent issue of *House Warmers*. Notice how Alan uses that newsletter recipe I just described.

How Dry Clothes Can Lead To Heating Problems

(Alan begins by saying, You have a problem, and here's what it is.)

*Take a look around the back of your clothes dryer. If you're like most folks, you'll probably find a half-dozen stray socks, a bushel basket-full of toys, and a **lot** of lint.*

Lint hangs around a laundry room like a prisoner looking for a way out. Notice how it always heads for the exhaust fans? If you remove the fan's cover, what do you find? Lint! And lint can hurt your heating system.

(Next, he explains what's <u>causing</u> the problem.)

*Ever give any thought to how an oil burner operates? It has a fan, a **high-speed** fan, and it has a powerful pump. It uses the pump to inject liquid fuel at very high pressure into a narrow pipe and out through a stainless-steel nozzle. The hole in the nozzle is only about as wide as a human hair.*

When the oil comes flying out of that nozzle's pinhole it's moving at the speed of a jet airplane. It immediately breaks up into a fine mist and mixes with the huge volume of air that's blowing down the burner tube, courtesy of the high-velocity burner fan.

At the same instant the oil and the air mix, about 10,000 volts of electricity jumps a gap between two electrodes situated a fraction of an inch from the nozzle's tip. The electrodes look sort of like the ones Dr. Frankenstein used. The white-hot spark snaps and instantly sets fire to the oil/ air mixture. In the average home, it's like having 7,000 books of matches flare up in less than a second, all under complete control. That's the tremendous power that quickly brings you warmth and hot water.

But try to imagine how an oil burner reacts when lint clogs its air inlet. The burner begins to "choke" because it can't get enough air for good combustion. The result? Not all the oil in the mist burns. Some of it goes up the chimney as smoke. That costs you money because you've already paid for that oil.

(Finally, he explains how his products and services can <u>solve</u> the problem.)

Now, we always check and clean your burner's air gate when we do our annual service, but you can help yourself by checking it every so often during the winter, especially if your clothes dryer is in the same area as the burner (check it when you're doing the laundry, it's easy!). Just look around the side or the bottom of the oil burner. If you see lint building up, just brush it off. Your efforts will pay off in lower fuel bills and you'll save yourself the inconvenience of a "no heat" call in the middle of the winter.

Some of the more-modern oil burners have a special fitting that makes them adaptable to an outside-air connection. We use these fittings to hook up a flexible air hose to the outside of the house. The kit is very similar to the exhaust hose on your clothes dryer.

With the outside-air kit, all the combustion air comes from outside the house. You eliminate your lint problem once and for all - as long as you don't have the air inlet hooked up right next to the clothes dryer's outlet, that is.

*But a **smart** oil heat company would **never** let that happen to you.*

Not bad, eh?

You can do this with any subject. You begin with a cluster diagram, and then lay the ideas out according to the recipe. Alan takes his customer through a discussion of a problem/solution, and he keeps it *totally* in the customer's self-interest. By doing this, he also effectively diffuses a common problem the customer might otherwise blame on the oil he sells to them. And all the while he's doing this, he's also drumming up new business.

This is one of the reasons why Alan Levi, Ace Troubleshooter and Wet Head, is so successful.

Here, take a look at how Alan used *House Warmers* to handle another difficult situation. A few years ago, we had a ridiculously mild winter here on Long Island, and when you're in the business of selling fuel to keep people warm, warm weather will have you reaching for the antacid tablets. Alan's customers, on the other hand, thought the weather was just peachy! They didn't have to buy as much fuel.

Now, he could have grumbled his way to the poorhouse, but instead, Alan decided to turn his mild weather woes to his advantage. He figured that if the weather was going to be so pleasant in the middle of winter, he might as well let his company take full credit for it. He put his tongue firmly in his cheek and told a story about his father, Irving Levi (who regularly appears in *House Warmers*). Here it is.

When The Rooster Refuses to Crow...

My father Irving likes to dress in layers. Years of going in and out of the cold have taught him that this is the best way to dress for a damp, Long Island winter. Irving starts adding the layers right after Labor Day. First, there's this sleeveless cotton sweater that peeks out from under his sport coat like a breastplate. Next, comes the woolen sweater. A topcoat follows, and then a scarf and gloves, and, of course, the heavier trousers. By New Years Day, Irving can have more layers than an archeological dig.

Each fall, we watch Irving the way the folks who write the Farmers Almanac watch caterpillars. Irving's wardrobe provides the best long-range weather forecast around. Even the weatherman stops by now and then to see what Irving's wearing.

This winter, Irving has been wearing cruise wear.

But we knew this mild weather was coming. You see, last year Irving had more layers than an onion. Last winter, as you'll recall, New York was colder than Pluto. Irving saw it coming. He began to layer in mid-August. People were still sweating on the beach when Irving broke out that sleeveless cotton sweater. He had this faraway look in his eyes that made us all shiver. We knew we were in for a tough one.

On one particularly frigid day last February when the wind howled and it looked like even sunlight might freeze, Irving slid up the walkway, shook the snow from his boots, and said, "People need a break from this." I shrugged my shoulders. "What can you do about the weather?" I asked.

Irving just smiled. He had that faraway look in his eyes. "I'll see what I can do," he said, cryptically.

And that's why it's been so warm this winter. You see, my father Irving arranged it all. He's responsible for the mild weather. It hasn't been unusually warm because of a shift in the Jet Stream, volcanic eruptions, earthquakes, the fires in Kuwait, hair spray or the junk the astronauts left on the moon. It's unusually warm this year because Irving figured you needed a break. He just didn't let it get that cold.

Here's how he did it: When Labor Day arrived, Irving refused to put on that sleeveless cotton sweater of his. As a result, we had a very mild fall. As the holidays approached, Irving stuck to his guns. He kept the layers off and held winter at bay. For the same reason the sun won't rise if the rooster refuses to crow, the winter can't come if Irving refuses to layer. If you don't believe this, remember, the world once laughed at Galileo!

Anyway, Irving's planning to remove the few layers he's wearing sooner this year so spring will arrive ahead of schedule. This year, the Groundhog will look to Irving for guidance.

So as you burn less oil this winter and save money on your fuel budget, keep in mind my father Irving is responsible for those savings. Maybe you should send him a thank you card or something.

Alan's customers *loved* this story. Irving received hundreds of calls thanking him for all he had done for them. They needed a break, and Irving provided it. The customers *really* appreciated what he had managed to do!

And I really appreciate what Alan manages to do with his newsletter.

Newsletter Tips

Look around. How many people are reading over your shoulder right now? No one right? That's what I figured. You see, like most people, you like to read alone. That's why I write the way I do. I have never written to a group in my life because groups don't get together to read things.

I write to one person, and that one person is *you*.

Remember this when you're putting your newsletter together. Don't say, "Our customers tell us they like our speedy service," say, "You've told me you like our speedy service." Or better yet, "Mrs. Jones wrote me a letter the other day. She told me she really appreciated how quickly we got to her house when her boiler broke down. We had the new boiler in that very same day, and she mentioned how pleased she was with our clean work. We can do the same for you, you know."

See what I mean? Write to one person at a time, and speak plain-English.

Next, become a real person to your customers by telling them about yourself. In *House Warmers*, for instance, Alan Levi always saves a space to tell a story about his father or his brothers, who are also his partners. It may be something whimsical, it may be something that happened years ago, or it may be a story of a successful job. By showing their customers the people side of the business, Alan's customers feel closer to them than they do to other companies. When a competitor calls one of Alan's customers with a lower price, the customer is usually reluctant to switch because of the personal relationship he feels with Alan and the Levi family. In large part, this is because of the newsletter. At the very least, the customers will usually call Alan or his brothers, Richie and Marty, to discuss the deal they have been offered. And that's when the guys get a chance to ask the customer why he would ever consider doing business with someone else. If it's a question of price, Alan and his brothers talk *value*. If it's a question of a comfort-related problem, Alan and his brothers fix it. They don't let customers slip through the cracks.

At one point, Alan used *House Warmers* to publish a Bill of Rights for the company's customers. It went like this:

Your Bill of Rights

- You have the right to a comfortable home

- You have the right to a hot shower.

- You have the right to individual temperature control throughout your home.

- You have the right to a quiet heat-distribution system.

- You have the right to a comfortable level of humidity in your home.

- You have the right to a heating system that doesn't dirty your home.

When a customer calls to say her rights are being violated, Alan, his bother Richie, or one of the service technicians will go find out why. Almost always, this call leads to a sale because they get a chance to explain to the customer why they're having the problem.

If the house isn't comfortable, it may be because the boiler is too small or the system is out of balance. If they can't get a hot shower, they'll benefit from a new indirect water heater. If they don't have individual temperature control

throughout their home, they'll be receptive to a discussion of zoning. And so on.

You don't have to spend a fortune to drum up new business; your existing customers are your greatest resource.

12

You Must Make Money!

This is a pretty basic business concept, but it's often overlooked when things get competitive. You can get lots of work if you drop your price low enough. Everyone in town will want to do business with you, but you won't make any money - no matter how hard you try. If you're losing money on every job, you will *not* make it up on volume. Trust me on this, okay?

It's important to know your selling price, and I have no intention of getting into that in this book. There are people who are far smarter than I am when it comes to this, and they run seminars that you should consider if you don't know your selling price. Check out Maurice Maio and Frank Blau's courses. They're well worth your time.

Once you figure out what you need to keep your company healthy, don't drop your price in the face of competition. Instead, sell value and those intangibles we've been talking about. Explain *why* your price is higher than your competitors. Give them good reasons why they should do business with you.

And don't beat yourself up by believing that price is all that important. Here, consider what this guy had to say.

"If You Don't Have The Cheapest Price, You Lose!"

That's what the guy said to me. He looked me right in the eye and said, "If you don't have the cheapest price, you lose!" Them he crossed his arms and planted his feet. "And I know what I'm talking about because I've been doing business in this town for twenty-two years," he continued, "People buy *solely* on the basis of price."

"You mean you have to have the cheapest price or the home owner won't deal with you?" I asked.

"That's right," he said. "If you don't have the cheapest price, you lose."

"Well, I think that's amazing!" I said.

"What's amazing?"

"You've been in business for twenty-two years and you've consistently had the cheapest price. That's wonderful! How do you do it?"

He looked at me if I had lost my mind. "I *never* have the cheapest price!" he shouted. "That's the point. I always *lose* to the guy with the cheapest price."

"Oh," I said, honestly confused. "Then how have you managed to remain in business for so long."

He gave me a self-satisfied grin. "By fixing the other guy's crap," he said.

"You mean you follow the low bidder around and fix what he puts in?"

"That's right," he said.

"Let me make sure I understand this," I said. "The home owner gets a price from you and the other guy. Your price is too high so they hire the other guy."

"That's right."

"The other guy does the job?"

"That's right."

"Do they pay him?"

"Yes," he said.

"And then the job doesn't work and they can't get recourse from the other guy because he's the low bidder, right?"

"Once again, that's right."

"So they hire you and you straighten everything out?"

"Yes."

"Do they pay you?" I asked.

"Of course they pay me! You think I'd fix that bum's crap for nothing?"

"So they pay both you and the low bidder?"

"Yes."

"Add those two numbers together and tell me what you get," I said.

"Huh?"

"The two prices," I said. "What they paid the low-bidder, and what they paid you. When you add them together, do you still have the low bid?"

"I never thought of it that way," he said.

That was the problem. He wasn't thinking of it the right way. People don't buy the cheapest price; they buy value. And it's your job to explain how you add that value.

How My Brother-In-Law Managed To Go Out Of Business

He's pretty handy, my brother-in-law. He fixes just about everything around his house, so when he lost his job as a school principal he figured he would just take a ride down to Town Hall and apply for a contracting license. You don't need much to qualify as a home-improvement contractor here on Long Island; a few bucks for the licensing fee does the trick.

He was going to be a vinyl siding installer, my brother-in-law. He had a truck, a ladder, and a good eye for straight lines. He figured the rest would come easily - as long as his price was right. He figured if he could make a few hundred bucks a day, he'd be in great shape. He saw that couple of hundred as pure profit. He didn't worry about expenses because he already owned the truck and the ladder. He knew there wasn't much to the contracting business. You just had to make a couple of hundred a day to be in good shape. He'd get what he could in cash, and that would be even better.

We got together one weekend and he told me he was starting a job in this fancy neighborhood.

"How'd you get the job?" I asked.

"I knocked on the door and gave them a great price!" he said.

"What's a great price?"

"I'm doing it at my cost, but I figure it will get me into the neighborhood. You know what I mean?"

"I'm not sure I do," I said.

"Well, I'll put up my sign in front of the house. The people already told me I could do that because I gave them such a great price. When the neighbors drive by, they'll see the sign, and ask me for a price to do their houses."

And that's exactly what happened. People drove by, saw his work and his sign. They called him later that day and asked for prices, which my brother-in-law cheerfully gave. He quoted these folks a lot more than he had quoted the customer whose house he happened to be working on, of course. He had taken that first job at cost just to get into the neighborhood. Now that he was actually *in* the neighborhood he figured he was going to make a killing.

The neighbors took his prices and got on the phone with the guy whose house my brother-in-law did at cost. "This guy's price seems high," the neighbors said. "What's he charging you?" And when the first guy spilled the beans the neighbors got back on the phone with my brother-in-law and called him a thief.

"We want the price you gave the first guy!" they shouted. "Our houses are exactly the same! We're calling Consumer Affairs!"

"So what did you do?" I asked my brother-in-law.

"Well, I dropped my price, of course," he said. "I couldn't charge them as much once they found out how the first guy was paying. I wasn't looking for trouble."

"You mean you're going to take these jobs at cost?"

"Well, not exactly. I'll make a hundred bucks a day," he said. "That's not bad. Most of it is tax-free, and besides, I need the work."

And that's how my brother-in-law went out of business. He forgot that when you're in business you <u>must</u> make money. He got into the neighborhood, all right. *Everyone* wanted to hire him. They just didn't want to pay him a lot of money. And since he had no idea how much money he should be charging he went along with them. He worked seven days a week, and still managed to go out of business.

I saw a sign in a neighborhood store that was locked up as tight as a Mosler safe. The sign read, WE UNDERSOLD EVERYONE.

At least *that* guy learned his lesson.

Pulitzer's Prize

In 1883 Joseph Pulitzer came to New York City from St. Louis and bought the *World* newspaper. He set the price at one penny, which was half the price of two of New York City's largest, and more reputable, newspapers, the *Sun* and the *Tribune*. Almost instantly, the circulation of the *World* increased to 100,000 daily copies.

In a panic, the two larger newspapers dropped their price to one penny in order to compete. In one day, this made Joseph Pulitzer's *World* equal in stature to the *Sun* and the *Tribune*.

Companies that advertised their products in the *Sun* and the *Tribune* began to suspect that at a penny a copy, these newspapers were reaching people who didn't have the money to buy what their companies were offering for sale. You see, by dropping their price, the *Sun* and the *Tribune* managed to remove the value which advertisers had placed on these higher-end newspapers. Almost immediately, they began to pull their ads, and this led to a financial disaster for the two larger newspapers.

That left the *World* in a position where they could safely raise their prices, which they did, of course. Joseph Pulitzer was in the neighborhood.

So now let's say you're a Wet Head doing high-quality work. You're providing people with comfort and economy and you're delivering value by selling *comfort*, not equipment. Suddenly, you're faced with a competitor who quotes a low-ball price. But he's no Joseph Pulitzer, is he? This guy is dropping his price because he doesn't know his costs. He's just trying to undercut you, and he'll keep trying to do that until he puts himself out of business.

You have two options. You can meet the competitor's price. And keep in mind that by lowering yourself to his level, you are actually *elevating* him. And all he has to do is drop his price again - which he will do.

And then what will you do?

Your other option is keep your price, which you *know* allows you to make a decent profit and remain in business. You then explain to your potential customer the reasons why it is in their self-interest to deal with you. You go over their needs. You discuss their problems. You explain how you have the solutions that will deliver the best long-term value, and that this, too, is in their self-interest. You back this argument with testimonials from other customers, with your reputation as a Wet Head who knows how to deliver the goods. You stay positive and wildly enthusiastic. You show no fear.

There is never a reason why you should have to drop your price to a point where you cannot make money.

When you're faced with a challenge such as this, I invite you to use these two letters to help tell your story to that customer. *Never* give up.

We're Probably Not the Low Bidder

Good morning! Here's my company's proposal. It covers everything we discussed as well as the alternates for the additional work you said you would consider. We're probably not the low bidder on your job, and I want to take a few minutes to explain why.

Most heating contractors buy their materials from a plumbing and heating wholesaler right here in town. We all pay the same prices. Our wholesaler stocks material that falls into the "good," better," and "best" categories. You'll recall we talked about this when we discussed your job. If one contractor's price is lower than another's the difference is probably not coming from the cost of the material, unless, of course, the low bidder isn't dealing with a legitimate plumbing and heating wholesaler.

Some low bidders buy their materials from a home center. Home centers run sales on "loss leaders" every week. Low bidders see this as a way to shave a few bucks from the cost of the material. You could go to the home center and get the same price on that "loss leader" if you wanted.

We don't buy from the home center. We prefer to get *all* our material at the plumbing and heating wholesaler because they carry a full line of top-quality, heating equipment, things you can't find at the home center. We support our local wholesaler because they're essential to our ability to give you great service. When we need something special, or an oddball part in a big hurry, these guys will drop what they're doing to service us. The home center won't do that for us, nor will they do it for the low bidder. We've found it pays to develop a good relationship with a full-line supplier.

A customer we'd quoted called us recently for help. He had hired the low bidder to do the original installation, but now he had a problem with the product. Rather than take care of his problem, the low bidder told the customer to call the home center. He tried that, but got a run-around. The contractor told the customer he didn't have time for problems, and besides, how could he expect good service when his price had been so low. We took care of that family, and we charged them a fair price.

If you find our price is higher than the low bidder's, make sure they're offering you the same material we discussed. Make sure they're not cutting corners by eliminating components or substituting cheap material.

Remember, a car may be a car, but a BMW is very different from a Yugo. Be a wise consumer, and keep in mind, if we're all getting our material from a legitimate source, we're all paying the same price. If there's a wild difference in our prices, that difference *has to* be coming from someplace else.

Maybe the low bidder has simply decided to work for less profit. Maybe he figures he can make it up on volume. We see that business philosophy in a lot of places nowadays.

But the low bidder has to pay the same price for a truck as we do. And gas is no cheaper at his gas station than it is at ours. Quality tools cost money, so does liability insurance, workman's compensation, the cost of clean uniforms, drop cloths and safety equipment. These bills *must* be paid.

Many low bidders have no idea what their operating costs are. They've never taken a business course, and they live from job to job. As a result, many of them go out of business. If you have a problem a year or so after the installation, there's a good chance the low bidder will be gone, or operating under an different name. Either way, you're stuck with the problem.

The difference between our price and the low bidders' has to be coming from someplace. Chances are it's coming from his mechanic's salary; low bidders usually pay their mechanics less than we do. After all, they're the low bidder.

Low bidders generally have a tough time attracting skilled craftsmen. Skilled craftsmen earn good wages because they work neatly and quickly and they know exactly what they're doing. We'd send nothing less than a skilled craftsman to work in your home. Would you expect anything less?

Low bidders typically hire people with limited experience. These novice mechanics are willing to work cheaply because they have little or no training. They need on-the-job experience. Unfortunately, they want to get it on *your* job.

Low bidders don't allow much margin for error. If there's a problem, low bidders return to your home reluctantly, and usually because you threatened them. More often than not, you wind up with a patch job, performed by an angry, surly man who resents you, even though you hired him and paid him promptly.

Low bidders usually don't have any sort of support staff. If you call with a question, you get to speak to an answering machine, at worst, or an answering service, at best. Rarely will you get someone who can answer your technical or billing questions competently and on the spot.

Since the low bidder doesn't know his real cost of doing business, he won't set aside money to replace or repair that old truck or those old tools. The result? You're home waiting for him to show up, but he's broken down on the road with no way of getting in touch with you. He has no car phone. He has no two-way radio. He has no support staff. He's the low bidder. He can't afford these business tools.

The low bidder sets no money aside for the future. He lives from job to job. He often falls behind on his payments to his suppliers. They cut him off and he's forced to make excuses to you. You can't have your new boiler or water heater or whatever because "the manufacturer didn't ship on time," or "the truck broke down," or "there's a strike at the factory." You'll just have to wait . . . or you'll have to pay him the full price in advance, and in cash. And don't be surprised if he uses this money to finish his last job, rather than start yours.

The low bidder rarely takes time to read or do research or attend educational seminars. He's too busy running around trying to make a profit by losing money on each job. He's not really interested in the latest products and technological advances. He has no time to learn new things. He thinks "plain-vanilla" is good enough for you. He won't take the time to show you a menu of products, nor will he consider how your comfort needs can best be served in the most economical way. He'll just ask what you want, and then give you a low-ball price.

The low bidder may not have a good relationship with the local code officials. Years of cutting corners under various company names have probably made the inspectors wary of this guy. They'll go over his jobs with a fine-tooth comb, and often insist he redo things. He'll resent this, and he may ask you for more money after he's started your job. He might even put you in the middle of the argument with the inspector, and perhaps even the local utility.

And while all this is going on, your heating system will be laying dormant. After all, if the low bidder can't afford to do the job right, he certainly can't afford to do the job twice.

We're probably not the low bidder on this job, but I assure you we *have* given you our best price for the value we offer. And when you need us in the years to come, we'll be there to serve.

Thanks for your consideration.

(This letter will also help you make your case when you're battling price.)

You May Be Wondering
How We Arrived at the Price of Your Job

Good morning! And thanks for giving us the opportunity to make a proposal on your new heating system. We realize that at times like these people in our trade often speak a language other than plain-English, so we'd like to take a few moments to explain how we arrived at the price for your project.

It began with a heat-loss calculation. You may recall we spent a good deal of time going through your home, measuring the dimensions of your rooms, windows and doors. We looked for fireplaces, exhaust fans, recessed lighting fixtures, and other things that can cause heat to escape from your home. We inspected the quality and quantity of insulation in your attic. We also asked whether you have had any additional insulation installed in your walls. These things can make a big difference in how much fuel you'll use, and what size your heating system will be.

We took the time to survey your home and perform an accurate heat-loss calculation because this *always* results in the greatest economy for you. We would *never* guess at how much heat your house might lose on the coldest day of the year. Nor would we ever base the sizing of your new heating equipment on what's already in your home. That's simply not good engineering. We can't take for granted that the long-gone contractor who first sized your heating equipment was correct. It *always* pays to check, especially nowadays with fuel costs so high.

And when we performed the heat-loss calculation on your home, we certainly didn't use "rules of thumb." "Rules of thumb" often make the sizing process easy for a heating contractor, but these overly conservative rules also are *guaranteed* to increase your fuel bill every winter from now on.

Most of the "rules of thumb" we've run across in our travels come from the days of single-pane-glass windows, little or no insulation in the walls or ceiling, open-window ventilation, and cheap fuel. We refuse to provide you with an oversized heating system, and that's why we always take the scientific approach.

And nowadays, the science is pretty advanced! We've invested in both computer hardware and software that help us do our job of sizing your system quickly and accurately. The system we're proposing will fit your home like tailor-made clothing rather than something off the rack. There is **no reason** to increase your long-term fuel bills by oversizing, and that's why we began your project by sizing it accurately.

Next, we've made sure the radiation we'll be placing in your home is sized to your home's needs, and is also pleasing to look at. There are many ways to heat a home nowadays, and we considered all our options before putting your price together. We may even propose a hydronic *radiant* heating system for your home, and if this is the case, you'll *feel* the comfort, but you'll never see the radiators!

We've also engineered your new system into "zones" so that you can heat your home according to the way you live. You'll be able to keep different parts of your home at whatever temperature you choose. We may even have proposed a "Smart System" that keeps track of outdoor weather conditions and adjusts your indoor comfort from moment to moment. Having a "Smart System" is like putting a cruise control on comfort!

What you find in our proposal is the best possible combination of efficiency, economy, durability, and style. And as we install it, we promise to be as meticulous in our workmanship as we've been in preparing this proposal. The people we will send you will be professional heating technicians. They'll have years of experience installing accurately sized systems just like yours. They'll take great care and pride in the work they do in your home.

In putting this price together, we considered the training that went into the preparation of these valuable people, and the salaries and benefits we pay them. We knew you wouldn't accept anything less than the best technicians. Our people have graduated from technical schools sponsored by the manufacturers of the products we're proposing for your heating system. They know these products inside and out, and they understand how to meld them into a system designed to provide you with long-term economy and unsurpassed comfort.

Our people also regularly attend industry trade shows. These shows allow them to monitor, first hand, the rapid advances in heating technology. If a new product has been proven in the laboratory, and in the field, and if it enhances our "systems approach" to heating, we will consider it, test it, and then offer it to you. Our proposal contains several such cutting-edge heating products.

In designing your system, we've also given a great deal of thought to any service it might need in the future. We want to make sure your future service contractor will have easy access to all of your new system's components. We also checked with our supplier to make sure they would have parts on hand for these components as time goes by. We never include in our proposals any cheap, fly-by-night products that may be here today and gone tomorrow. That wouldn't be in your best interest.

In selecting the components for your heating system, we've consulted our friends within the local and national trade associations to which we belong. We regularly attend meetings with these people, and we gain by their experiences, as they gain by ours. By networking with others in our industry, we're much better able to offer you the most trouble-free equipment available.

We'll be buying this equipment from a reputable suppler with whom we've had years of business experience. We know they stand behind the products they provide - as will we.

When we were through designing and engineering your system, we totaled the costs of labor and material, and then we included a fair percentage for profit. As we have in the past, we'll invest a good portion of this profit back into our business. By doing this, we'll ensure that our company remains healthy, and that we'll be there for you in the future.

All in all, this price represents the best combination of first-cost and long-term operating cost. And while you're profiting by the savings your well-engineered heating system will provide, you'll also be enjoying an unsurpassed level of comfort.

Thanks for giving us the opportunity to explain how we arrived at this price, and, within the coming days, for letting us show you how *very* good we are

What Did You Pay For That Bush, Mister?

You know, people will *pay* for value. Wet Heads help people perceive value in everything they do. I had a call once from a heating contractor who told me a home owner spent $15,000 landscaping his new home, and then balked at the price of the heating system the contractor had proposed.

"The trouble is the neighbors can *see* the landscaping? They can't *see* the heating system," he said.

"Can't they *feel* the heating system?" I asked.

"Yeah, but that's not the same," he said.

"We have *five* senses, you know."

"But it's easier to sell something you can *see*," he insisted.

"What about Calvin Klein?" I asked. "He sells perfume for a whole lot of money. He advertises it on TV. He has skinny people who look like they've snorted all the cocaine in Columbia slinking down a long white corridor. No one can smell this stuff, but they rush to the store to buy it anyway."

"They buy that because the neighbors can *smell* it," he said.

"Okay, how about these knuckleheads who sell these New Age CDs? They get people to shell out twenty bucks for the sounds of whales doing the deed and rain falling on aluminum siding. What about that?"

"They play that stuff when the neighbors come over," he said. "The neighbors can *hear* it."

"Ruth's Chris Steak House gets people to show up, wait hours on line, and then shell out like fifty bucks for a piece of meat. They do this by telling you how good it's going to taste. You're working with the sense of touch. Can't you make a case for a hydronic radiant floor? You ever stop to think what people can *do* on a warm floor?"

He went back and sold the guy that hydronic system. He was able to do it this time because suddenly he *believed* in what he was doing, and because he got excited about what he was selling. The neighbors might not be able to see it, but they sure can *feel* it.

Never let price stand in your way. The stuff you sell costs more because it delivers the goods. Be proud of your price, and then make your case for pure creature comfort

What could be more in that customer's self-interest?

13

In The Customer's Self-Interest

We begin with a tale that's painfully personal.

They built the house we're living in in 1950 and they gave it a copper-in-concrete radiant heating system.

In 1970, the previous owner of my house noticed wet spots on his kitchen floor and knew that the family budget was about to take a trip down Hershey Highway. There's not much you can do when the copper in the concrete begins to dissolve.

So the guy called a heating contractor who came in and pronounced the radiant floor heating system dead. The contractor gave the guy a price to convert to copper fin-tube baseboard. And then he did what every heating contractor on Long Island does, which is to run copper fin-tube baseboard everywhere there was a wall. He skipped only the front and back doors because they don't make baseboard with hinges. And needless to say, he used no dummy cover. Every foot of that loop was live element. Why did he do this? Because this is the way he was taught to do it. The method is known as a Long Island Heat Loss Calculation. Everyone here uses it.

When its time came, the upstairs portion of my house, not coincidentally, was sized using the same method, so I now am the proud owner of 200 linear feet of 3/4" baseboard. If you ever need any, give me a call.

You know what got me thinking about this? The other day, a heating contractor I know let me in on the way he does a heat loss calculation.

"I go around and measure the radiators," he said.

"You mean on a steam system?" I asked.

"Not just steam," he said, shaking his head. "I do it on *every* system. You gotta support the radiation, you know."

"I agree with you in the case of steam," I said. "With steam, you have to match the firing rate to the connected load because steam is a gas that wants to condense. If you have more metal than steam, the steam won't make it to the end of the run and you'll have a cold house. But I think you're making a mistake if you size a hot water boiler that way."

He shook his head. "Nope, that's the way I do it. Been doing it that way for years," he said righteously.

"But you're probably going to oversize the boiler if you measure the radiation on a hot water job," I told him.

He just shook his head from side to side. "Works for me," he said. "Been doing it this way for years."

"You have to do a heat loss calculation when it comes to hot water heat," I continued. "That's all that matters. The heat loss."

He kept shaking his head. "Takes too long to do a heat loss calculation," he said. "Gotta get on to the next job. Much easier to measure the radiation."

So I invited him over to my house for a beer.

"What's the heat loss of my house?" I asked after we'd had a couple of cold ones.

"You're gonna make me work?" he chuckled.

"Not work; I'm just curious. How would you size this house? C'mon, show me."

He got up from the couch, tugged up his pants and went out to his truck. He came back in a couple of minutes with a tape measure, a pad and pencil and a calculator. He laid the tape around the perimeter of the house - both upstairs and down - and he recorded the numbers. Then he added it all up.

"You got 200 feet of 3/4" baseboard," he said.

"I know."

"Each foot of three-quarter puts out 580 BTUH when the water's 180 degrees," he said.

"I know."

"So two-hundred times five-eighty is a hundred-sixteen-thousand. That's the heat loss for your house."

"That's what you'd quote me on? If I called you for a price on a replacement boiler, I mean."

"Yep," he said. "Plus the domestic hot water load, of course. You have an indirect water heater, so we'll have to add quite a bit for that."

"Come here for a minute," I said as I walked him into my office. He rolled his eyes and followed me, shaking his head all the way.

"You're gonna show me I'm wrong now, right?" he said. "You're gonna whip out some book or something and show me how what I've been doing for all these years is wrong, right?" He laughed and shook his head again.

I didn't say anything. I just turned on my computer and called up the heat loss calculation software program I use. It's called Calc-Plus and it's written by a guy named Ed Horgan. It's real easy to use.

Ten minutes later, I'd sized the whole house for the heat loss on a 15-degree day.

"The heat loss is forty-thousand BTUH."

"It can't be," he said, shaking his head with conviction. "Not with all that radiation you have." He shook his head again. "*Can't* be. You'd *never* support the radiation with that small a boiler."

"So in other words, you'd put in a boiler four times bigger than what the house actually needs?"

He waved his hand at the computer screen, dismissing it. "I don't need any of that technical crap," he said. "You just match the radiation, that's all. You *gotta* support the radiation. It's there in the room!"

"But radiation *isn't* heat loss," I said, trying my best to convince him. "Your price is going to be out of line if you base your boiler size on the radiation. It's not in the customer's self-interest."

He just kept shaking his head. "Been doing it this way for years," he said. "I'm not about to change now. I'm not putting in something that's too small. Not me. I don't need problems."

Whenever my friend loses a job he blames it on the price. "Hydronic is just too expensive," he says.

Smart Wet Heads regularly beat him up.

Smart Wet Heads know that radiation is not heat. Heat is what they have to put into the house to overcome heat loss. If they put in too much heat, they know they'll be wasting their customer's money and short-cycling the boiler. Neither of those things is in the customer's self-interest.

When a smart Wet Head comes across an over-radiated house he'll use it to his advantage by accurately sizing the boiler, and then running it on a lower temperature. That saves the customer money - both short-term and long-term. This is especially true if you can put the house on continuous circulation with an outdoor-reset control.

Here's an example of what I'm talking about. Let's say you have a room with a heat loss of 5,800 BTUH. If the installer put in 10 feet of 3/4" baseboard and supplied it with 180-degree water, he'd match the heat loss on that cold day because 3/4" baseboard puts out 580 BTUH when there's 180-degree water flowing through it.

But suppose the installer put in 15 feet of 3/4" baseboard instead of ten. With 180-degree water flowing through it, 15 feet of 3/4" baseboard will put about 8,700 BTUH into the room. That's way too much - even on the coldest day of the year. The burner will cycle too often, and combustion efficiency will suffer. That's *not* in the customer's self-interest.

But since this "extra" baseboard is already there, a smart Wet Head will make it work to his advantage. Here, consider what happens if you run 150-degree water through that baseboard. At 150 degrees, each foot of 3/4" baseboard will put out 380 BTUH. Since you have 15 linear feet, you'll be emitting 5,700 BTUH into the room. That's just about right for the coldest day of the year. It costs less to operate at 150 degrees than it does to operate at 180, right? *That's* in the customer's self-interest! Just pipe the new boiler with primary/secondary pumps to eliminate the possibility of flue gas condensation and you're all set.

A smart Wet Head will discuss these things with the customer right up front. The Wet Head's price will be more attractive. The customer's fuel bills will be lower. The level of comfort will be much higher. The baseboard will be quieter because it won't be expanding and contracting as much, especially if the Wet Head puts the system on continuous circulation and outdoor reset. The lower temperature will also keep the burner from starting and stopping as often. That means higher efficiency.

When you present value that is in the customer's self-interest you will be irresistible. Smart Wet Heads use every tool at their disposal to do this, and the heat loss calculation is one of the first tool they'll reach for.

Fast Heat-Loss Calculators

There are a bunch of heat-loss software programs on the market, but my all-time favorite is Calc-Plus by Horgan Vertical Applications Corp. (HVAC). It's very easy to use, even if you're not a nerd. The program does heat loss and heat gain at the same time. It sizes baseboard by brand for you, and even tells you how many end- and corner-caps you'll need. It gives you an easy-to-follow print-out that you can use in your presentation to your customer. Great stuff!

Heat loss is different for hydronic radiant heating systems because the air temperature at the ceiling stays so cool, and there are very little convection currents in the room. Because of these differences, tubing manufacturers such as Wirsbo and Heatway have developed software that is specific to hydronic radiant heat.

Make The Most Of Mechanical/Electrical Time Capsules

At some point down the road, someone is going to have to service the equipment you install. Smart Wet Heads discuss this with their customers and help them plan for the future by giving them a mechanical/electrical time capsule - to be opened in times of trouble.

Picture this. You're sitting with your customer, going over her comfort needs and planning her project. You take out a folder from a job you recently completed. The folder contains a piping and an electrical schematic of the job along with a description of how the system works, including the control strategy. There are photographs of the job before, during and after. If the job had hydronic radiant tubing, there's also a videotape record of what the floor looked like before you covered the tubing.

You explain to your customer that records such as these are in her self-interest because you may not be the contractor who services her hydronic system in the future (although you'd very much like to be). These records will let any future contractor know exactly how her system works and how you installed it. It will give her peace of mind, and it's one of the many things your company does that makes you different from your competitors.

Price doesn't have to be that big an issue. Not if you present your case in the customer's self-interest, and that's what smart Wet Heads do on *every* job.

Picture Perfect

If you're doing a job that's especially sexy it would pay you to hire a professional photographer to take photos. You will, of course, have to get the customer's permission before doing this, but most people are flattered because they're proud of their homes.

Why would you pay a professional photographer? For the same reason why you want your customer to hire you. Sometimes it just doesn't pay to "do it yourself." A pro can make both you and the job look great, and when you include these photos in future presentations your customers will know you take enormous pride in your work.

Which you do, right?

It will cost you a few hundred bucks, but it's money well spent because very few heating contractors are willing to make this investment. Be different. Choose a few great-looking jobs, put those records together and you'll have an award-winning presentation you can use for years to come.

How To Compete With Lazy Heating Contractors

There are three claims that I've listened to for years. Lazy contractors use these claims to get out of having to convince people that hydronic heat is in their self-interest. You'll be competing with lots of lazy contractors so you should be aware of these myths.

1. Americans don't want to spend money on their heating systems because they move every seven years.

My parents moved my brother and me from New York City to Hicksville, Long Island on a summer day in 1957. Hicksville is Mayberry with a temper. I lived in the same ranch house until I married The Lovely Marianne in 1972. During the years I spent in Hicksville, only two of our neighbors moved away. They were replaced by people who looked just like them.

When we returned from our Florida honeymoon, where I managed to give the rental car to a young thief, The Lovely Marianne and I moved into a brand-new garden apartment. The apartment had virgin walls, shag rugs, and a furnace. This was also the year I became a devoted Wet Head. We lived with that cursed furnace for 1,108 days, and finally broke our lease so we could move into an apartment that was blessed with hydronic heat.

I worked a full-time job during the day, and two part-time jobs at night and on the weekends; Marianne worked full-time as a key-punch operator. We saved every week, and on a hot, humid day in July, 1977, we moved into our first home, where we remain to this day.

During the 19 years we've lived in this blue-collar neighborhood, only two homes have changed ownership. I've known my neighbors longer than I've known my four daughters. Most of the neighbors are good friends; others we tolerate. On hot, humid summer nights we sit outside, drinking cold beer and swatting mosquitoes. We all know each other's relatives. We borrow tools from each other, which we rarely return, but no one keeps track. The same mail carrier delivers the mail six days a week; the same newspaper guy delivers *Newsday* before we awake each morning. It is a good place to be.

One morning, *Newsday* carried a story under the banner, "It May Be an Empty Nest, But Seniors Want to Keep It." The story cited a survey of 1,300 seniors conducted by the American Association of Retired People. It told a story I instinctively already knew. AARP found that 81 percent of the over-50 crowd wanted to stay right were they were, and for the rest of their lives. More than three-quarters of the seniors (76 percent) wanted to live with "people of all ages" rather than be surrounded by fellow seniors.

This didn't surprise me because my 76-year-old father recently complained that I had seated him with "old people" at a 75th birthday party for The Lovely Marianne's mom. If I had to guess, I'd say my father was the oldest coot at that table, but that's not the way he sees himself. In his mind, my father is still fighting in the gin mills of Manhattan's east side. In his head, he is forever young.

The *Newsday* survey also noticed a growing interest in reverse mortgages, which allow home owners over the age of 62 with low or no mortgage debt to convert their frozen home equity into cash through open lines of credit or loans secured by their homes. Reverse mortgages don't have to be paid off until the senior moves to another home (less likely nowadays), or dies.

I take this as an indication that folks have more money to spend on comfort in their golden years than most contractors think.

Now, I'm no expert in demographics, but most of the people I meet have neighbors who have been there a lot longer than seven years. Like me, the people grumble about the guy next door. "When's Jim gonna fix that upstairs window?" they say to each other. "It's been broken for ten years. That bum should do something on the weekends besides fish and watch football!"

Like me, they've complained about Jim and his busted window, but they've also watched Jim take his kid to Little League practice. They've watched that kid leave for college. They went to the kid's wedding, and now they complain when Jim's grandchildren run across their lawns.

And on hot summer nights, they all share a cold beer.

Does your neighborhood look like this?

Call me a rebel but I can't buy into this myth that Americans don't care about their homes because they're constantly moving. I think it's a crock. It's a story for lazy contractors who don't want to take the time to sell-up and market their services like professionals, and it's a story I'm not buying.

I firmly believe the average American *will* invest in hydronic comfort if they know about it. It's in their self-interest. Lazy contractors don't bother trying; Wet Heads do.

2. Consumers won't buy hydronics because they want air-conditioning.

This is like saying, "People won't buy hydronic heating because they want plumbing." In fact, I think I can make a better case for this second ridiculous statement because at least hydronics and plumbing both involve pipes. What the heck does heating have to do with air-conditioning?

Here, you're a professional so I'll assume you know how to do a heat-loss calculation. I'll also assume you know how to do a heat-gain analysis for the purpose of air-conditioning. The loads you arrive at will be different, right? You know this because you do these calculations all the time.

Now, try to get these dissimilar loads to travel well through a single network of ducts. You know what's going to happen.

First, you have to decide where to put the ducts. If you put them in the ceiling you'll be favoring the air-conditioning over the heating because cold air is heavy and it sinks. If you put the ducts in the floor, you'll be favoring the heating over the air-conditioning because hot air is light and it rises. Either way you chose, your customer will sacrifice comfort for a good part of the year.

Living on Long Island, where we can fill a tumbler with water by waving it through the thick August air, I know that air-conditioning is more about humidity control than it is about blowing cold air on people. Ductwork is fine for air-conditioning.

But heating should be about warming the surfaces around those people. We do this so the people will lose less heat from their bodies during the winter when the wind blows hard across the icy Atlantic. You simply can't do a good job of warming the surfaces of a room by blowing scorched air out of ducts. It's crude.

But most Americans don't know this. Because of the post-World War II tract housing boom the average American thinks it's normal to have scorched air vomiting from ceiling-mounted registers. They put up with drafts and extreme changes in room temperature because they think this is normal.

How fortunate you are to be a Wet Head! You can offer your customers year-round, luxurious comfort. All you have to do is separate the heating from the air-conditioning by selling them two *properly* sized systems.

All you have to do is show them what normal *really* is.

3. *Hydronics is too expensive.*

Here's an analogy I'd like you to take to your next customer. Let's say you have a choice between two cars. One is a new, fuel-efficient model, the other is a Chevy Impala that has been driven by an angry manufacturers rep for the past 20 years.

The new car is going to cost more to buy than the Impala, of course, but the Impala is going to use more fuel, and it's *certainly* not going to be as comfortable to drive.

Which will your customer choose?

Now, if you use the logic lazy heating contractors employ, the customer will chose the Impala every time because it's cheap, and it will probably get them where they're going.

Would you agree with that?

Oh, I know, I know. You're going to tell me that people spend money on cars because the neighbors can *see* the car. Cars are status symbols. People can't show off their heating systems to their neighbors.

Wanna bet? Ever watch the way neighbors react when they walk into a house graced with, say, hydronic radiant floor heating? If those folks live in scorched air territory, they get all limp and silly when they hit those gloriously warm floors. They smile big, wet happy smiles.

Don't tell me you can't show off your hydronic heating system.

But that aside, try another analogy. Build two identical houses, side by side. Install a modern hydronic-radiant-heating system along with a split- or high-velocity air-conditioning system in one. Give the other house a cheap furnace with low-budget central air system.

From what I've seen, if you size and install everything properly, the first house will probably use nearly 40 percent less fuel each year while providing a much higher level of comfort.

Okay, which house will the public buy? Lazy contractors believe the public will choose the scorched air house because it's cheaper. But what do *you* say?

You know what I say? I say that buyer is going to pay for the hydronic system even if she *doesn't* have it installed. She'll pay for it every month in her fuel bills for as long as she owns that house. She'll never know it but her average monthly fuel bill will be nearly twice what it might have been. She'll never know this because the average contractor won't tell her. She'll think her high fuel bill is *normal.* Imagine that.

Throw in the life expectancy of a furnace and a water heater compared to a boiler and an indirect heater. She'll have to replace the equipment, right? Who pays for that?

Suppose you showed her how a hydronic/air-conditioning system could be paid off as a part of her mortgage. Spread the few extra thousand dollars now for the superior system and spread it over 20 years. It disappears, doesn't it? It also gives her certain tax advantages, doesn't it? It makes sense, *doesn't it?*

I'd like you to keep focusing on this truth: *She will pay the extra cost one way or another.* Her only choice is whether she will make her payment to the mortgage company, and be done with it in 20 years - or to the utility company where the payment is subject to world-wide, commodity-market fluctuations, and is never-ending.

It's her choice. But it's *your* job to explain it to her.

Comfort Is In The Customer's Self-Interest

Comfort, after all, is what people buy. If you approach *everything* you do with this in mind I guarantee you will sell more hydronic heating systems. Even though they seem to cost more, but they really <u>don't</u> - as you just saw.

When you focus on comfort, you focus also on *value.* A contractor from Montana wrote me a letter not long ago. "Electricity costs five cents or less in this part of the country," he said. "You can heat the average home electrically, and spend less than a thousand dollars on the installation. It's very hard to crack this market with a hydronic job that might start at eight-thousand dollars. Of course, you haven't experienced discomfort until you've lived with electric baseboard, or even worse - wood heat!"

To which I say, Amen!

If you were going to live in a home for years you'd pay a bit extra going in for comfort, wouldn't you? So will your customers. It's in their self-interest. But you have to do a good job of telling your story.

In the case of the Montana contractor we were talking about an extra seven-thousand dollars for the hydronics. When you average that out over the life of a 20-year mortgage you're talking small change. Especially if you consider the value hydronic heat adds to a home when and if the owners decide to sell.

But most important, during the years they live there *they will be comfortable.*

So we're talking seven-thousand dollars. Big deal. What will these people spend on cars over the next 20 years? What will they spend on appliances? How about vacations? At thirty bucks a month, they'll spend more than that on basic cable TV over the next 20 years.

Are we really talking about a lot of money here? Seriously.

I'm telling you, the problem lies within the contractor who decides up front that people are cheap and that the difference between scorched air and hydronics is an overwhelming amount of money. There is nothing any of us can do for that contractor. He has beaten himself before the conversation even begins.

You have to *sell* comfort. And people are willing to *buy* comfort because it is in their self-interest. It really is.

Feeling Is Believing

It helps, of course, if you have a way to show your customers what hydronics feels like, especially hydronic *radiant* heat. Ideally, you can heat your office with hydronics as my friend Alan Levi, Ace Troubleshooter, did. Or you can build a moving showroom out of a van, as my friend Dennis Bellanti suggests, and had done.

If you don't want to go to that extent, you can do something even simpler. Emerson-Swan, a manufacturers rep in New England, came up with one of the neatest ideas I've ever seen.

Because they represent Heatway, they wanted to have a way to show what hydronic radiant heat feels like when they were working a trade show. They built a two-foot-square box out of plywood. It was about six-inches high. They divided the top of the box into four sections. On each square foot they installed a different flooring surface. One section was tile, another was hardwood, a third was a thin carpet, and the forth was clear plastic so you could see the Heatway hose they'd attached to the underside of the floor.

Next, they got themselves a plastic watering can, just like the ones garage mechanics use to top off your car's radiator. They cut a hole in the side of the can and installed an electric immersion heater. They caulked around the hole so it wouldn't leak. When they plugged in the heater, the water would get very hot, so they installed an aquastat in the other side of the can to limit the maximum water temperature. It was a very crude "boiler," but it did the trick.

They used a tiny submersible pump to substitute for a circulator. They attached one end of the Heatway hose to the pump's discharge, and let the other end of the hose run back into the watering can. They purged the water through the "system" and started it up. Within a half-hour, their "floor" was wonderfully warm to the touch. And the people at the trade show couldn't keep their hands off of it.

The whole works couldn't have cost them more than a few hundred bucks, but what a display they had!

In Canada, the Canadian Hydronic Council's built themselves a similar rig, but it was much more elaborate. They, too, use their display at trade shows. It works on the same principle, but theirs has an actual (electric) boiler. Picture a cube measuring about five feet on each side. You'll need a forklift to move this thing because it weighs an awful lot. When you remove the padlock, the top of the cube flips up and becomes a large sign inviting you to experience hydronic comfort. The front of the cube flips forward and down, exposing a radiantly heated floor. Each side of the cube swings out. On one side is a radiant panel-type radiator, on the other is hydronic baseboard. The boiler sits in the center of the cube and provides the warm water.

They've been showing this hydronic cube at trade shows for the past few years and they always have a line of people waiting to slip off their shoes, step up, and experience the comfort.

See? If you want to do something to convince your customers of the value of hydronic comfort, you can. And you don't have to spend a fortune.

Remember, *feeling* is believing.

14

Getting Sharper

We use these padded envelopes to ship our books all over the country. I buy the envelopes by the case from a local company and I always want to be the one to go and pick them up - even though I can have them delivered, and even though I can send someone else.

I want to pick up the envelopes because this is the *best* use of my time.

I first sit with the company's slick catalog. There's a message from the company president right there in the front of the catalog. He promises me great service and a fair price. He shows me photographs of his massive warehouse and tells me he will always have what I need in stock.

I find what I need and call the company. I always get voice mail.

After spending a few minutes in that loop, I get to speak to a customer service representative. She's never heard of me, even though I do business with these people all the time. Once she finds me on the computer she gets the prices wrong.

After we work all of this out, I drive the ten minutes to the place and walk in the front door. I stand at a little window and watch a half-dozen women eating. They're always eating at this place, no matter when I arrive. No one gets up to help me. They look at me and at each other. They whisper to each other. Sales people walk by and they look at me as well.

Finally, one of the women will slosh over to me and ask what I want. She has a mouth full of cream cheese. I tell her I phoned in an order, but this means nothing to her so we start all over again. Who am I? Do I have an account with them? What's my salesperson's name? Do I know the price I'm supposed to pay? Do they have the envelopes in stock? What's the capital of Bolivia? Who pitched in the third game of the 1950 World Series?

I answer all these questions as best I can and they tell me to drive around the back, which I gleefully do because "around the back" is by far the most interesting part of this place.

I walk in and I'm met by a half-dozen smoking, cursing warehouse employees who ignore me because they're eating. It's break-time. No matter when I go around back, it's break-time. They talk about what a jerk the last guy who picked up his order was. The aisles are clogged with debris. The paper envelopes are within inches of the ceiling-mounted gas-fired unit heaters. There are centerfolds from girlie magazines hanging on the walls. Everyone's cursing and spitting on the floor.

They pull my order when they are good and ready to do so. They try to do wheelies with the fork lift. Half the boxes they bring me are busted so I refuse them. They go back to get more, taking their sweet time. No one ever offers to help me load my van, and they always blow smoke in my face when I'm signing the ticket.

This is the *best* use of my time because it forces me to think about my own business and how people see us.

If there was anywhere else to buy envelopes locally, I would *still* buy from these guys because of the great lessons they teach me over and over again.

You should have such a place to visit. It is positively inspirational.

The Most Important Person In Your Company

I think the most important person in your company is the person who first answers your telephone. You know why this person is so important? Because this is the first person the customer talks to. This person is more important to your company than any salesperson, manager, technician, installer, or even the owner because *nothing* happens until someone answers that phone.

Most one- or two-person shops use answering services. If you use one of these, call them frequently and see how long it takes for them to pick up. Listen to what they say when they do pick up. I have a friend who once used a service that was based 1,000 miles away from his office. "It's the Nineties!" he told me. "The answering service could be anywhere. And I got a good price."

The person answering his phone had a back-woods southern accent that sounded like a mixture of Jack Daniels and pork bellies. She couldn't pronounce his very ethnic name. She'd try two or three times when she picked up the call, and then finally wing it. She never said it the same way twice. She was talking mostly to people from New York who have their own troubles speaking English. It was a disaster.

But he got a good price.

If you use an answering service, have friends call and pretend they're potential customers. See how the service treats them. This could be one of the best things you ever do because nothing happens until that phone rings. And the person who answers that phone is the most important person in your company.

Most larger contracting companies will hire someone to answer the phone. You know how they select this person? They hire the first bozo who walks through the door and agrees to work for hardly any money at all. It goes like this:

Manager: "What should we offer the new receptionist?"

Owner: "Offer her squat. All she's got to do is answer the damn phone, for Pete's sake! It doesn't take a college degree to do that."

Manager: "You're right. How's minimum wage sound?"

Owner: "Minimum wage sounds good. Offer her minimum wage. That way, there's more money for me!"

That's the typical hiring process when it comes to the most important person in the organization. It's being repeated all over America, even as we speak. If you've ever made a phone call, you know it's true.

Anyway, time goes by and this second conversation takes place between the manager and the owner:

Manager: "She's been with us a year. I think we should give her a raise."

Owner: "For what? All she does is answer the phone."

Manager: "I'm afraid if we don't give her a raise she'll leave. Then we'll have to look for someone else. Let's give her a dime more an hour. After all, she's been here a year."

Owner: "But all she does is answer the phone! Any idiot can answer the phone."

Manager: "I'd hate to have to train a new person."

Owner: "What's to train? She picks up the phone, and she transfers the call. I gotta think about this."

Will she get her dime an hour more? Maybe. And maybe not. Either way, she's going to be miserable.

Now consider this. She is the first person the customers will speak to when they call, and she's mad as hell because she has this dead-end job.

Try giving her a call sometime. It's quite a learning experience.

"Hello? Joe's Plumbing and Heating, please hold," she drones.

So you hold. You hold for a long time. And then, just as you're about ready to give up and hang up, the most important person in the company barges back into your life.

"Are you holding?"

"Yes."

"Please hold."

"Okay," you say to the dead line.

Several minutes later, the voice, sounding as though it was dredged from an old cesspool, returns. "Hello, Joe's Plumbing and Heating."

"Hello, may I please speak with Joe?"

"Please hold."

"But . . . " Too late! She's gone. You start cleaning your fingernails. You put your feet up on your desk. You wait. You listen to the annoying on-hold radio station as it plays music you despise. You listen to the head-banger music the most important person in the company has selected for the on-hold portion of your experience. You sit on hold. Time passes. The earth turns on its axis. Seasons come and go. Farmers plant and harvest grain. Babies grow in their mothers' wombs. Glaciers melt.

"Hello, Joe's Plumbing and Heating."

You jump to your feet. "Can I pleeeese speak with Joe?"

"Joe ain't here. You wanna talk to his voice mail?"

"Can't you just take a message?" you plead.

"Please hold."

You are in telephone purgatory. The Japanese tried to call America once in 1950. They couldn't get through to any of us so they built an entire industry geared toward the needs of people who were on hold. As you read this book, at least half of the people in the country are on hold. I'm serious. Look around your office right now. Do you see what I mean?

So you wait. And then, without coming back on line, Joe's Plumbing and Heating's most important employee switches you into the psychotic maze that is voice mail. Voice mail is there to help the most important person get her job done. Voice mail costs a few bucks, but hey, levels of aggravation that are this exquisite don't come cheap!

By the way, the voice-mail salesperson sold the system to Joe in person because he couldn't get through to him on the phone.

Voice Mail speaks: "Hello, you've reached the phone mail system. Please dial your party's extension number and then pound on your phone."

You don't know your party's extension number. You pound on your phone anyway. That breaks the connection, and now you have to call back.

She answers.

"Joe's Plumbing and Heating."

"I was just cut off."

"Please hold."

She comes back on after what seems like a month. Before she can speak you blurt out, "Lemme speak to someone in service."

"They're out to lunch," she says.

They're not the only ones out to lunch.

The Operations Manual:
A Recipe For A Successful Company

That company I just told you about was in trouble because no one took the time to teach the most important person in the company how to answer the phone.

So she made it up as she went along.

If you run a heating company one of the scariest things you can do is ask a group of employees how they perform a routine task, such as answering the phone, dealing with an accident, or installing a boiler. Chances are, you'll get as many different ways to do it as there are employees to ask. Some of your people may be doing that routine task in a way that violates state, federal and moral law while making you liable for everything that's gone wrong since the Garden of Eden.

"Gas leaks? Oh, I always use my Bic lighter. Finds 'em right away!"

Stuff like that doesn't happen as readily to companies that use Operations Manuals. Everyone does everything the same way, and they make a lot less mistakes. A good Operations Manual can be a cookbook for business success if you take the time to put a good one together.

I few years ago, I worked with Alan Levi, Ace Troubleshooter, on an Operations Manual for his company. It was a tremendous learning experience for everyone involved - especially me.

What we wound up with was a huge document that clearly defines every single aspect of Alan's business, and lays out every job that every employee does. Nothing was left to speculation or chance.

It took us nearly two years to put the thing together because we were starting from scratch, but it was well worth the time invested. To give you a sense of why I say that, take a look at just this tiny part of his company's Operations Manual.

Installation Procedure for Hot Water Boilers & Burners:

- The Installation Manager will arrange the needed material for the Installer before the job.

- The Installer must check the contract and pay close attention to any special instructions and/or cautions.

- The Installer must enter the house through the correct door. This information will be on the contract.

- The Installer must cover and protect the customer's floors and staircases before moving any equipment in or out of the house.

- The Installer must read the job's Instruction Sheet and always keep it with him on the job.

- The Installer will arrange all the needed parts at the truck. The Helper will carry these materials to the work area and organize them safely on the floor near the boiler.

- The Installer will take the old boiler apart.

- The Installer should take care when draining the system water. Try to have the water as cool as possible. The Heating Engineer is responsibility for calling the home owner and asking them to shut off the burner before the Installer arrives. Never drain hot water into a customer's toilet. Never pump old system water onto the customer's lawn or flower bed. Never pump old system water into a customer's slop sink without first asking permission.

- After draining the system, flush the drainage area with fresh water.

- The Installer or Helper will vacuum the old boiler thoroughly.

- The Installer or Helper will clean the chimney base and smoke pipe. The company makes plastic bags and plastic sheets available to reduce the spread of debris in the customer's house.

- Some boilers have to be cracked (cast-iron) or cut (steel horizontal-tube) before they can be removed from the job. A Certified Dismantler will cut old steel boilers into pieces small enough to be hand-carried off the job. There are times when we will remove the old boiler after the new boiler is installed. The Helper will stand ready with a fire extinguisher while the Certified Dismantler works.

- The Installer and Helper will bring the new boiler into the boiler room. The company has a motorized hand truck for this purpose.

- If the boiler has four or more sections, the Installer should split it before bringing it into the house.

- Before reassembling the boiler, the Installer will clean the nipples and ports. Use Real-Tough as a boiler sealant.

- The Installer will tighten the tie rods evenly.

- The Installer will position the new boiler in the place selected by the Heating Engineer and the home owner.

- If possible, the Installer should show the home owner where the new boiler will be and how much room it will take up.

- The Installer should always keep future service in mind while he's installing the boiler and hydronic accessories.

- The Installer will place the boiler on blocks and install the steel near-boiler piping.

- Once the steel piping is in place, the Installer will level the boiler. Use only steel shims for leveling.

- The Helper will set up the burner and oil lines while the Installer is setting up the boiler.

- The Installer will consider the smoke pipe before connecting the waterside of the system. He should use as few smoke pipe fittings as possible.

- The Installer will always use isolation valves on each zone.

- We recommend each Installer follow the piping diagrams shown in Dan Holohan's book, *Pumping Away.*

- Before filling the system with water, the Installer will check the radiator air vents to make sure they're working. If possible, the Installer should try to do this before starting the job. It is easier to check air vents when the system is under system pressure.

- Once filled, the Installer will purge the system of air.

- The Installer will do a complete combustion efficiency test on the new burner. He will leave a completed efficiency test sticker on the boiler.

- The Installer or Helper will paint all the bare pipes black.

- The Helper will clean up the work area. Always leave the place cleaner than you found it.

That's just a tiny piece, and it leaves no doubt as to what Alan expects of his people. It takes them from one step to the next and removes any question as to who's responsible for what. When new people join the company, they get a copy of the part of the Operations Manual that is specific to the job they'll be doing. If they have any questions, they just look it up. If their supervisor isn't around, they know what to do. If there's an argument, the Manual usually settles it.

I want to tell you how we put this together, and then I'll tell you how you can get to the same place we did with a lot less pain.

Lots Of Clusters

We began with a series of cluster diagrams. We had one that laid out all the employees by job definition. Next, we made clusters that broke down each job into the dozens of tasks these people routinely performed. Finally, we took each task and further clustered it into all the things that might possibly happen while the employee was doing that particular task. As you can imagine, some of these clusters were very large.

From the clusters diagrams we came up with a series of questions. For instance, when we were talking about how to install a hot water boiler, we asked questions such as, What happens if the Certified Dismantler is taking the old steel boiler apart and he accidentally sets something on fire with his torch? Well, someone should be standing by with a fire extinguisher while he works, right? Who should that be? We decided to give that job to the Helper.

Now, who provides the Helper with the fire extinguisher?

And who's going to be in charge of making sure the fire extinguisher is available?

Who takes care of checking to see that all the fire extinguishers are full, and meet the Fire Department's standards?

And if the Fire Department comes to check the fire extinguishers, who should speak to them?

What if that person is out sick that day?

As you can see, it gets complicated, but think of all the things that could go wrong if one or more of those links in the chain of events broke.

The chances of this happening are much less once you have an Operations Manual. We came up with hundreds of questions we had to ask. They fell naturally into categories and we separated them into long lists.

Dozens Of Meetings

We next scheduled meetings with key people to discuss each topic. We made sure we picked people who represented all sides of an issue. For instance, the day we discussed boiler installations we had a company owner, a heating engineer (their company's name for a salesperson), a few installers, a helper, the installation manager, and a service technician. These are all the people who would normally be involved in a new boiler installation. We got together in a conference room and shut off the telephone. I set a tape recorder in the middle of the table so no one would have to take notes. Then, we took one question at a time and picked it apart until no one had anything else to say. Each meeting started at 8 AM and ended at Noon. We did this dozens of times.

No comments or questions were out of bounds during these sessions and there were a few days when the conversations got heated, especially when we realized how many different ways there were to do a routine task. It was a real eye-opener, and everyone learned a great deal. Some people, for instance, had little tricks they used to save time and money. They thought everyone knew these tricks and were surprised to learn that we didn't. These good ideas eventually became a part of the Operations Manual, and company policy.

You unearth a great deal of good information when you take your company through this process. It is a *major* brain-drain. It's time-consuming and sometimes painful, but it's well worth it.

The ground rule was that we stick to the specific topic. There's a tendency to go off on tangents when you put any group of people together for four hours, and it was up to the moderator (that being me on most days) to keep the group on track.

We wouldn't leave a subject until everyone agreed that we had come up with the best way to do this particular task. This is important because once it becomes a part of the Manual, you want everyone to feel as though they were a part of the decision, otherwise they might second-guess the Manual later on.

As I said, I tape recorded each session to save time. I made it clear that the tapes were for my purposes only, and that I would use them later on to make notes. This put everyone at ease, and after fifteen minutes or so, everyone forget the tape was running and let loose with what was on their minds. Boy, did they let loose!

When the meetings were over, I worked with the tapes, turning them into rough-draft notes for management's review. They took my notes and added their input. I edited these and sent them back for a second review. Again, management made their corrections.

When we had the final draft, management distributed the appropriate sections to each employee, but not before meeting with them and going over each point. Each employee then signed a form saying that they had received their copy of the Operations Manual and that they understood their responsibilities.

A Book You *Must* Read

Probably the most important business book I have ever read is *The E Myth Revisited - Why Small Businesses Don't Work and What to Do About It* by Michael E. Gerber (HarperBusiness: ISBN 0-88730-728-0). Mr. Gerber draws this important distinction between working **in** your business and working **on** your business.

He tells a story I've seen so many times. A contractor gets fed up working for the boss so he decides to go out on his own. He winds up creating a job rather than a business. He works twice as long for the same money he was making before. He can't figure out what he's doing wrong, and within a couple of months or years, he goes out of business.

Mr. Gerber has a *very* important messages to give Wet Heads. I can't possibly tell it as well as he does so I urge you to pick up a copy. It's not a long book (264 pages) and it will probably change the way you do business forever.

Please read it.

Dale Carnegie *Works*

As we come to the end of our talk I want to recommend one other thing to you. I took the Dale Carnegie course in 1971 when I was 21 years old. My old boss, George Wallace, sent me, and for that I will bless him forever.

That first night in class the instructor asked me to stand and say my name and what I did for a living. I found this painful. Twelve weeks later, they couldn't sit me down, and I haven't sat down since. Dale Carnegie is not just about speaking to groups of any size, it's about enthusiasm and confidence. No matter how old you are, you can benefit from what these people have to teach.

I recently sent my daughter, Kelly, through the course. We decided to do this during the summer between high school and her first semester at Notre Dame. She came out of that course a different person. When she got to South Bend she just looked around and took over.

This course will have an unbelievably powerful impact on just about everything you do in business. You'll make some valuable contacts because these courses attract people from all walks of life.

It is tailor-made for Wet Heads because Wet Heads, above all others, must remain positive and wildly enthusiastic.

So just do it.

15

You Don't Have To Beat The Bear

Two guys are hiking in the woods when they come upon a big black bear and her cubs. The mother bear gets up on her hind legs and lets loose a horrifying growl.

One of the guys strips off his backpack, takes out a pair of running shoes and quickly laces them on. "What are you doing?" the other guy says. "You can't beat a bear. It's impossible!"

"I don't have to beat the bear," the first guy answers, standing up. "I just have to beat *you*."

For years, people have told me that I'm out of my mind to try to compete with scorched air. "Those systems are cheap!" they say. "People won't pay a higher price for something they can't show the neighbors. Hydronics is just too expensive. You're wasting your time."

I've never paid much attention to those people. I just watch my friends go out and sell hydronic systems - radiant and otherwise - to home owners and get their price on every job they bid. These guys don't quit when told they can't do it. They Just Do It.

They're not trying to beat the bear. They're not trying to convert *the whole country* to hydronic heat. They're just beating the other guy to the business - one job at a time.

They're able to do this because, in most case, the other guy has already decided the customer can't afford hydronics. "I'm not gonna suggest that stuff," he says. "It's too expensive. And besides, people change houses too often in this country. And no one's gonna pay good money for something they can't show to the neighbors."

These guys have a thousand reasons why they can't get the business. They talk themselves out of the business before they even step into the arena.

You don't have to beat the bear. You just have to beat *that* guy. And that's not hard to do because that guy has already beaten himself.

Decide what business you're *really* in, and figure out who your customers are. Put your plan together, and begin to market yourself in the customer's self-interest. Don't try to change the whole world; just go after one job at a time. Do this and you *will* beat that other guy. Not every time, but often enough for it to have a *powerful* impact on your business.

Keep that crazy Canadian, Lord Sanford Fleming, in mind the next time you go to see a customer. He changed the way the entire world tells time, and he did it in just a few years by being irresistibly persuasive and by presenting his case in the customer's self-interest. You can do the same.

My daughter, Kelly, and her classmates got 40,000 people to form a wave that flowed in two directions at the same time one magical Saturday afternoon in South Bend,

Indiana. It crested and pounded around a noble old arena for five magnificent minutes that will burn brightly in my memory all the days of my life.

You can do *anything* you set out to do as long as your goal is reasonable, and you *really* believe you can do it. Stay positive. And *never* give up.

www.ingramcontent.com/pod-product-compliance
Lightning Source LLC
Chambersburg PA
CBHW060544200326
41521CB00007B/472